L.A.'56

ALSO BY JOEL ENGEL

L.A. '56

A DEVIL IN THE CITY OF ANGELS

JOEL ENGEL

Thomas Dunne Books

St. Martin's Press

New York

This is a true story. Much of the dialogue is recreated or imagined based on established facts, contemporaneous accounts, documentary evidence, and interviews. Names of some characters and other identifying details were altered, as per agreements with certain sources.

THOMAS DUNNE BOOKS.
An imprint of St. Martin's Press.

L.A. '56. Copyright © 2012 by Joel Engel. All rights reserved. Printed in the United States of America. For information, address St. Martin's Press, 175 Fifth Avenue, New York, N.Y. 10010.

www.thomasdunnebooks.com
www.stmartins.com

ISBN 978-0-312-59194-6 (hardcover)
ISBN 978-1-250-01245-6 (e-book)

First Edition: April 2012

10 9 8 7 6 5 4 3 2 1

To my wife, Fran, who has endured the relentless click-clacking of a keyboard lo these many years without ever telling me to get a real job

ACKNOWLEDGMENTS

Special thanks to Joseph P. Bonino, former commanding officer of the LAPD's records and identification division.

I also want to recognize Glynn Martin, executive director of the Los Angeles Police Historical Society, and in fact the whole organization.

Deep gratitude for the woman at the Los Angeles County Archives, who managed to come through for me each and every time no one else could.

Tips of the hat to the librarians at the California State Archives and UCLA's University Research Library.

Sincere appreciation to the present and former residents of South Los Angeles, who shared memories and showed me around town. Same with the cops and private investigators, who offered insights and direction.

A martini or two to master storyteller Harold Livingston for reminding me what to leave out.

Deepest thanks to Teri Denise and Toni, the daughters of Todd Roark, for being so kind under difficult circumstances.

Speaking directly to Tom Dunne: Thank you, sir, for recognizing a

viii

viii

 Acknowledgments

great story and standing behind it, and for running the best little imprint this side of anywhere, the aptly eponymous Thomas Dunne Books.

To my editor, Brendan Deneen, I'm grateful for your smarts, your taste, your dedication, and your deft touch. Oh, and for your extraordinary editorial assistant, Nicole Sohl, who makes things happen that otherwise seem impossible.

And of course, I owe this whole book to Danny and Margie Galindo.

LOS ANGELES, 1956

CHAPTER ONE

Willie Roscoe Fields stops hammering for a moment and wipes his brow. It's hot in South Los Angeles in the summer, especially on the tar-paper roof of a new house. Still, this is nothing compared to the cigarette-tip heat back home in Louisiana. In California, no matter how hot the day, the cool evening breezes change the tune. They always remind him of how good it feels inside a woman. But then, so had the sweaty bayou nights and the cold and the rain and every other kind of weather. Everything reminds Fields of poon, and when you're talking to him and he drifts off for a moment, as he usually does, you can bet he's lost in thoughts of dipping his wick in some well—maybe the woman's across the street, the one who stiffed him up just by walking by. *She doesn't know what she's missing,* he thinks, and that's how it starts. *If she knew, she'd be happier than any woman alive* and could never live without that good thing he can give her whenever and wherever she wants it. And she'll want it all the time and everywhere. Because to have Willie Fields do you is to pop your cherry all over again.

Too bad some women don't know what that kind of happiness is worth. Like Linda Harris, the pretty young lady who recognized him on a Los Angeles street in the heart of black L.A. seven years ago.

"Ain't you from New Orleans?" she asked, stopping him as he smiled at her when they passed each other crossing Central Avenue and Thirty-ninth.

He doesn't like remembering that day anymore, and in fact forgot about it long ago, but at the time he thought she'd pegged him as the real deal. He gave her that big I-like-what-I-see-and-I-think-you-like-what-you-see grin and said "Yeah, I am" on the assumption that his reputation had preceded him; either they'd met before or she'd recognized him as that big, handsome, hung stud everybody was always going on about. At least in his mind.

Linda told him what a happy surprise it was to run into a familiar face, a friend of a friend of a friend from the same neighborhood, especially since this was only her second week out here and she was feeling kind of lonesome and homesick and overwhelmed by so many people going to and fro.

"It's like Mardi Gras here all the time," she said. And compared to 2 million strangers, Willie might as well have been an old dear friend.

"How long you been out here?" she asked.

"Since the war. I was in the army, in Europe."

True, Fields had been a soldier. And yes, he'd been mostly on the West Coast since the fighting ended. But he'd never made it to Europe, never fired his rifle at a German. He'd gone AWOL after basic training at March Field, down in Riverside, looking for action in a part of the world where big black men wandering around out of uniform in white cocktail lounges may as well have had neon signs flashing ARREST ME on their foreheads, so he spent most of 1944 in the stockade. The army, wondering why the hell this moron hadn't been weeded out at the induction center—even considering he was a Negro—discharged him on a Section 8. And if you asked Fields why the military cut him loose without a trial, he couldn't tell you the reason, which pretty much explains the Section 8.

"Oh, goodness," Linda said. "You weren't wounded or anything, were you?"

"Oh, no, nothin' too serious."

"And so once the army discharged you, you just stayed out here."

"Yeah, guess so. Just stayed."

Like a lot of other young men assigned to California bases, Fields had come to believe home was the past, California the future.

Linda said, "I talked to a lady the other day that told me she used to recognize almost every face she saw on this street. Now she feels like a stranger in her own city."

Being black, Fields didn't have much choice but to locate himself in that part of L.A. where he was supposed to be—he and thousands of others with the same skin color. It was the kind of migration that had already been going on all over the country for decades. Negroes wanting to make a living and raise families and reduce their odds of swinging from a willow tree had been fleeing Jim Crow for points north and west, with most settling in New York and Chicago and Detroit and Philadelphia and a few other cities. But in Los Angeles before the war, there hadn't been a sudden wave as much as a steady trickle, slow enough to allow for smooth absorption in this new place where both Negro newsweeklies, the *Eagle* and the *Sentinel,* devoted half their pages to society doings and churchgoing. The war changed that. These new fellows, too many were bad apples.

Old-timers on Central Avenue had begun complaining about all the "low-class Negroes" crowding their streets, fighting and whatnot, forming gangs, not dressing properly, driving Cadillacs they couldn't afford. It was polluting their little bit of paradise from the way it had been when people behaved themselves and went to church and worked hard and listened to the sweetest jazz and blues this side of Harlem in smoky dark nightclubs up and down Central. And the police left them alone. Mostly. Now there were more cops than ever, sometimes even for good reason.

"I know a juke," Fields volunteered.

"Yeah, that sounds fine. I could use to hear some music," she said.

He led her around the corner, where his '38 Plymouth Roadking was parked. It looked like it hadn't been painted since the day it was introduced, and some of the dents were from the owner before the owner before the owner he'd bought it from, but it usually started up and had plenty of room in the backseat for whatever he needed plenty of room for.

Linda climbed in and at first didn't wonder why they were leaving all the bright lights behind—the area where you'd think live-music joints would be—for the quieter streets of courtyard apartments and small homes on postage-stamp lots. She wasn't worried, though. In L.A., she already knew, the business districts and residential streets were mixed like squares on a big checkerboard. But then the Roadking slowed and Fields parked on a neglected cul-de-sac where the streetlamps managed only to flicker in front of an apartment building that hadn't been painted since the first war or had its lawn watered since the last rain.

"This is a nightclub?" she asked, not needing to.

"My place," he said, smiling, expecting her to be glad. "Let's have a drink."

"No, no drinks, I don't want to, I want to go back."

"Baby, you won't know what you been missin' till you had old Willie here."

"I won't be missing nothin'. Take me back."

But Fields didn't want to take her anywhere but inside, and if not there, then the car would work just fine. He wanted her naked, and he was going to have her, and she'd thank him for it later.

He grabbed her close and forced kisses on her face and neck, stifling her screams and fighting off her swinging arms with one hand while the other moved up her dress and between her legs. She slammed them shut, but he was so much bigger and made a fist, twisted it sideways, and cleared space in there. The ease with which he was gaining ground said that he'd had to do this before. ·

Linda kept looking for someone passing by but saw no one. Now, instead of trying to hold him off, she managed to poke him in the eye, which surprised him. She took advantage and jumped out of the car, then ran but without her purse. She didn't care. She just kept running, kicking off her heels and sprinting barefoot down the middle of the street and screaming.

For hurting him, and on general principle, Fields felt entitled to her wallet and watch.

Of course, Linda now knew where he lived and the car he drove.

When the police came calling, he gave his name as Thomas Adams but had a bank passbook with him that said James Lonnon. He tried explaining how he wanted to keep his various girlfriends from knowing where he was or with whom when he wasn't with them.

In any event, it was Willie Roscoe Fields who was found guilty of attempted rape and grand theft person, for which he was sentenced to all of ninety days in a county work camp and five years' probation, both the prosecutor and judge agreeing with the public defender that this young man was essentially good-natured but dumb as a shovel and could easily have misinterpreted a young lady's acceptance to go for a drive as something more. And she wasn't actually raped, was she? He hadn't even made it safely to third base. What good would be served by a long incarceration at state expense when a little education was all he needed?

Besides, the woman was black, not white.

Two years on, after moving to another boardinghouse farther away from his probation officer, Fields forgot one Tuesday to report. It was an honest mistake. And then when nothing bad happened, he decided it was too much trouble to keep checking in, and anyway why should he have to? He went back to New Orleans, got married, had a kid, left them and returned West, found another job pounding nails, then went back to New Orleans before trying L.A. one more time and finding this job that lets him drive the power buggy sometimes. It's a good job, a union job, and pays pretty well, but that's no big deal because he's always made a decent living, being big and strong and not afraid of hard work, especially if there's something to reward him later. Sometimes still he calls himself James Lonnon, sometimes Thomas Adams, sometimes James Leonard, depending on which bank account he deposits his paychecks to and which name people know him by. He might not remember which is which until someone shouts out to him.

One thing never changes. His best friend is always his "love rod," as he calls it. He sometimes stares down at it in awe, carrying on one side of the conversation but hearing the other, saying how it's just the two of them against the world. He believes he's been blessed with an ecstasy wand and doesn't understand why he can't make a living by using it, like those white men in stag films. It just ain't fair. Big as they are down below, those white fellas can't stand up to his three-hander. Nobody can. The way he figures it, if you want to do right by those women and all the people who pop to watch the films—if you want them to see a *real* show—all you got to do is put him naked in front of the camera and there'd be no need for any other men. He'll fill and satisfy all those actresses and never lose a minute in recovery, and then the word'll get out and pretty soon ladies who don't even do that for a living will line up to be in these films with him, and he'll be the king of the stags, and that'll make him richer than Rockefeller.

CHAPTER TWO

Los Angeles is a sad city. Standing on Hollywood and Gower, pretending not to be a cop, Danny Galindo tries not to notice how sad it truly is. As sad as all the dreams that die here—millions more than come true. He imagines he can see them hanging over the street like brown smoke. They choke your breathing and squirt from your lungs when you blow out. Or is that the smog? *Smog,* the new word a newspaper guy made up to describe the brown air that rolls by as thick as fog and hides the mountains just a mile away and the tops of the palm trees sixty feet up. Well, smog and sadness and palm trees go together. That's L.A.

People other places think it's happy here. They connect sunshine with feeling good, not understanding that you can get to resent it. But you can, just the way you do on those mornings when daylight floods through the blinds and pries your eyes open. That's how it works. Sooner or later, everyone who got off a train or Greyhound with big dreams that don't come true finds out how sad L.A. really is. There they are, guys with Purple Hearts from Guadalcanal working as cashiers at Clifton's Cafeteria for a buck an hour, and women who'd refused more than a kiss from their dates back home in Des Moines blowing someone in an alley for not much more, living in tiny, airless rooms five flights up in brick buildings that are one more small earthquake away from rubble. For them, daylight comes too soon and, unless they're tanked on cheap gin, night lasts too long.

That's why Danny tries not to notice, to not see too much. But that pain is everywhere. And he's a cop, a detective. It's his job to notice things he'd rather not notice. Especially this thing that's not good to know about people. It's what all cops eventually learn—something he learned earlier than most, just after that January morning in 1947 when some patrolman barfed up breakfast before calling in the nude woman's bisected body lying in a weed-filled lot down in Darkville, as other cops still like to call it.

It wasn't the fact of a murder, exactly, or even the particular gruesomeness of it. After all, no real imagination is required to appreciate that countless men are capable of depraved cruelty. There's never been a shortage of sickos out there, and from time to time one shows himself, as Danny realized in a night-school criminology class when he had to memorize infamous names and their gruesome deeds—for instance, William Edward Hickman, who in these same streets twenty years before had kidnapped and slaughtered Marion Parker, twelve years old, the daughter of his rich former boss, carving her up like a side of beef.

No, Danny had quickly learned what he wished he still didn't know when ordinary men with no connection to the murder of that young woman and no record of ever hurting anyone began crawling out of the sewers to confess to the murder. There'd been nearly 150 of them, of whom 38 spoke only Spanish. Which was why, only a year after he joined the force, the LAPD promoted its *pachuco* cop Galindo, the smartest, most elegant, most ambitious of a handful of Mexes in uniform at the time, and likely the only who'd ever sat inside a college classroom.

Not in Spanish, not in English, none of these confessors had done the deed. They couldn't provide any details beyond what the papers had already printed and couldn't describe the one essential that only three cops knew but hadn't committed to print—even on the police and coroner's reports—precisely because they knew some reporter would get his hands on it and incite yet more confessions. If it ever leaked that the young lady had been pregnant when she was sliced open, you'd have another two hundred guys trying to take the credit with no way to confirm whether they deserved to spend their last months in San Quentin.

Still, policy had to be followed, and policy says that every confession has to be taken, even wastes of time. Every *i* dotted, every *t* crossed. That's what William H. Parker pushed for when he was inspector and deputy chief, and what he insists on now, as chief of the department— especially when the press is paying attention. And for a long time after the Black Dahlia murder, they didn't pay attention to anything else. So the cops listened to the men and pretended to take them seriously and asked questions. Like *Why did you want to mutilate and murder this beautiful young woman?*

It made Danny feel dead inside to hear answers that were dipsticks measuring the depth of their worthlessness. When he excused these guys without an arrest, they begged him to believe that they really had done it, swear to God, cross their hearts, hope to die. Literally.

Imagine wanting to fry for a crime you didn't even get the pleasure—if that's the word—of committing; you didn't get to rape her, didn't get to slice her or chop her, didn't get to hear her screams or savor the terror in her eyes then watch the life go out of them; didn't even get to stand in the field and smell January's orange blossoms in the dawn breeze as you arranged the torso just so. True, maybe none of these men would've even gotten off on any of that. Danny didn't think any of them would have. But still, every one of them wanted to suffer infamy and death because being known as the Black Dahlia's butcher was as close as they were ever going to get in this life to mattering.

Knowing facts like that about people makes it hard to carry on with anybody who doesn't know them, too. That's why cops have bad marriages. Their wives live in gardens of ignorant bliss where their husbands eventually poison everything.

Danny sees that all the time, sees the divorces and tanking up at cop bars just to get the courage to go home, sees that it's better not to get too intimate with civilians. So why even try? He's thirty-five years old, a compact five eight and 160, with wavy hair and bedroom eyes, and he looks good. The ladies like him as much as he likes them, probably more. His dance card is never empty. But being in love—well, either he's never been there or he has and can report reliably that it isn't anything to build your life around. He doesn't know which is true but he suspects the latter, which is why he prefers carefully picking and choosing how people move in and out of his life.

Make no mistake, though, brown-skinned Danny Galindo has built a great life. He doesn't care, or frankly think about, that the only way it could be better is if he were white. Because at least he's not black. Mexicans have it hard in L.A., but Negroes have it hardest, despite this being California, not Mississippi. It's been that way since forever, but it got worse, not better, six years ago, in 1950, when Parker engineered a coup and began speeding the transformation of the LAPD from the country's most crooked big-city department to the least. Good luck with that, but it meant no one wasn't under suspicion.

Parker cleaned house pretty good, all right, and Danny made the cut, maybe because he was Catholic and Parker was Catholic, and Parker loved Catholics; maybe because Danny was a war hero and Parker fancied himself one, too. But more probably because Danny was clean and he was good and nobody even tried to say he wasn't.

Just like that, things started getting better for those who took pride in their work, city, and department. Then Parker began recruiting troops, some from the Deep South, and didn't insist that they holster their prejudices. Maybe he shares them, maybe he doesn't. But he sure as hell doesn't want what the Negroes are doing on their side of the tracks to spill over into white society. Which means there's the criminal-justice system and there's street justice—and if you're a Negro in Los Angeles, you're subject to both.

And so it is inside the department, too, as Todd Roark learned the hard way. A war hero and a good cop, he got fired for bouncing a check. Poor Roark. The brass claimed he'd kited it, but that was bullshit. What they really canned him for was dating a white woman after his divorce. A female desk sergeant in his division found out about it, and each time she saw him, it ate at her like drops of acid, maybe because she was interested in him herself and he wasn't interested in her. So she called it in upstairs, as if it were a 288 or something. It might as well have been. Roark had stepped over the line and had to pay with his job. So says Parker's unwritten policy. His cops are free to put the fear in some Reggie Johnson for sneezing without permission on Central and Forty-ninth, but out of uniform they better be moral saints. And ipso fucking facto, dating white women makes a black cop unfit to be an LAPD officer. No, you won't find that policy written down anywhere.

Policy would've put Danny in a bad dilemma if he were a patrolman driving with a white partner who likes rousting Negroes for walking too fast or too slow or just being in his sight line at the wrong time of day. He's not. He's a detective, a man who works with his brains instead of his hands and wears pressed shirts, silk ties, pleated gabardine slacks, and Ricky Ricardo jackets instead of a uniform. Some ladies think he resembles a movie star, though they can never put their finger on whom. That means his wavy black hair, flashing brown eyes, and bedroom smile would make him handsome enough to be a matinee idol if only people his color got to make a living that way in English.

Still, he's no stranger to Hollywood. When Jack Webb moved *Dragnet* from radio to TV in '51, Parker saw an opportunity and cooperated on the condition that his boys in blue look like everything flag-waving Americans expect their police to be. So with the LAPD behind him, Webb based his series on real stories that came out of real cops—the good ones, anyway—and as it turned out a lot of them, including Danny, were interested in writing down their stories for sale. The studio, Universal-International, had offered them night classes on storytelling and how to type out a proper treatment, and once or twice a season Danny sells stories he's lived and heard to Webb. Danny's one of Webb's favorites, always welcome to show up on the set and say hello. Webb, playing Sergeant Joe Friday, uses the names of real cops, and there's a running gag when a character tells Friday he's got a homicide and Friday says, "Give it to Galindo."

The money and notoriety give Danny cachet, entrée, and the scratch for nice clothes. A lot of places around town, he wouldn't have to pay full price for dinner. People know Danny, and Danny knows people. The white cops let him be, and some don't think of him as a Mex. He's just Danny. Not that he bends over for them. He doesn't. He just gives off an air that people trust, even cops who can't see a brown or a black man without thinking that the cemeteries aren't full enough yet.

Maybe that's what makes Danny good at his job, which is to solve murders and rapes. Or maybe that has nothing to do with it. But he *is* good. And he'd better be, because business is booming. Major crime is up more than 40 percent in just twelve months, and L.A.'s on target for more than a hundred murders this year—the most since, well, 1947. Must be all those broken dreams. Danny wonders if the city is in for another Black Dahlia scene, like a steam valve someone will turn to release the pressure and set things even again.

On this warm afternoon, homicide detective Danny Galindo stands on a Hollywood corner watching the smog and sadness roll by like a funeral cortége. The streets are crawling with ladies who didn't know that the party ended long ago and men who kept waiting for their big break, both hanging on just one more day, and a day after that, till years had gone by, every one of them filled with the kind of pain and disappointment that show up on the face before the owner can see them.

If Danny's hunch is right, the man he's looking for will soon stop at the Knickerbocker up on Yucca. The man either murdered a small-time bookie in the hills near Bronson Caves two months ago, or he saw who did. Danny will know which by whether the man tries to kill him. If he does, the man won't see tomorrow. And if he doesn't show up at all, then the man's skipped town, probably for good—and it's on to the next case. There's always a next case. Especially these days.

CHAPTER THREE

CROSS BURNED ON VERNON AVENUE

The sign of the cross, hate symbol of the Ku Klux Klan, was burned into the lawn of a Vernon Avenue real estate broker sometime Saturday night.

The flames singed the grass in front of James Sidney's real estate firm at 2601 W. Vernon Ave., sometime between 6:30 PM Saturday and 10:30 AM Sunday, when Sidney discovered the charred warning.

The arms of the cross were approximately 3 feet wide and 5 feet long.

Sydney said that in addition to the burning of the lawn, the flames destroyed large signs in front of the office. He estimated the damage at about $300.

He said he had been in his present location for a year, but that he had received no previous threats, warnings or indication of hostility.

He said, however, that some of the homes he has been selling have been in mixed neighborhoods in Leimert Park and that there has been some manifestation of resentment against Negroes moving into these areas.

He said that the police told him that from all the indications, the cross burning was not the act of juveniles. He said he believes it was a deliberate act intended to frighten him out of business.

—An article that appeared in the *California Eagle* but not in any white newspaper— not the *Los Angeles Times,* the *Herald-Express,* the *Examiner,* the *Mirror*—during the summer of 1956.

CHAPTER FOUR

"Get your big, black ass in gear and get that thing moving," the boss shouts.

Willie Fields is glad to be off the roof and back in the power buggy, but that doesn't mean the job has his full attention. With Friday quitting time an hour away, Willie Fields can almost taste it, his daydreams as vivid as hallucinations. A few bucks in his pocket and some eager poon. Paradise, man, paradise.

"And watch where you're goddamned going. Up there, you mighta killed yourself. In that thing, you could kill someone else."

A few weeks ago Fields lost his footing on the third floor, fell, hit his head on the pavement. Everybody gathered around, sure he was dead. Someone went to call an ambulance. Then Fields came to, if he was ever out, grunted, said "Whoa," stood, dusted himself off. Not a scratch on him.

"Shee-it," Darryl said. "Good thing he didn't land on his dick. He'd have broken every bone in his body."

Everybody laughed. Even Fields. It was a compliment, right?

Willie Roscoe Fields is proud of being the first in his family to finish the seventh grade. He'll tell you about how well he can read if the topic comes up. Matter of fact, it's about all that the guys at work know about him, other than he sings to himself in a nice voice and when he talks at all he talks only about women, and they're not women, which accounts for why he never asks any of them to knock off the day with a beer. That's just as well, though, since it could be awkward saying no thanks and it would definitely be awkward saying sure, Fields being not exactly the kind of conversationalist who'd bring something to the party with a bunch of guys who can talk the ears off a chocolate bunny, as Darryl, who's from Arkansas, likes to say. Still, they don't make fun of Fields, not the way they do old Lucius, who was both dumb and mean when he worked there. They trade stories about him, some of them maybe even true, like the one Wally told about the time Lucius supposedly testified for a friend in a lawsuit: "And that lawyer axed him whether he was sure he could see all the way to where George was standing, and he said, 'Yes, suh, I'm sure.' And the lawyer he said, 'Son, you mean to tell me that at midnight, in the dark, no streetlights, you could be standing more than a hundred yards away from the scene of the accident and still see every detail?' And Lucius say, 'Yes, suh, I can.' And the lawyer he say, 'Tell me, son, just how far can you see at night.' And old Lucius he thought a while and he say, 'Well, suh, I can see the moon. How far's dat?'" And the guys, they busted up laughing, but Fields didn't get the joke, so he asked what was so funny. "You are, man, you are," Wally said, not fearing in the least that this man who stood six four and weighed 250 with muscles the size of hubcaps had any sort of mean in him. No one had ever seen anything but his good side. Of course, none of them came built with a pussy, a booty, and two delicious jugs.

"Me?" Fields said. "I'm funny?" He likes that.

At five, Fields is first to pick up his check and hit the street. He drops into his green '51 DeSoto coupe, a little dented but nothing to be ashamed of for a five-year-old on only its second owner. All that chrome on the grill and bumper. One of these days he'll shine it up pretty. He's

only sorry he didn't buy the sedan, making it easier to get into the backseat if he has to, but the lines on the coupe were okay, and anyway he
was lucky to get this repo at the price when he saw it sitting on the corner at Jake's Car Auctions.

The car spits smoke as he turns south on La Brea, passing hourly
motels, liquor stores where the owners keep loaded pistols on their laps
behind the counter, ramshackle houses without lawns, and new store-
fronts that don't stand a chance. He pulls up in front of his credit-union
office, deposits the check for eighty bucks, takes fifteen in cash for the
weekend, and walks next door to Toots Barbeque Roost, gorging himself on a slab of ribs, pot of beans, and two malt liquors.

A copy of yesterday's *Eagle* is on the counter. He skips past the
front-page news about the NAACP confab held the previous week in San
Francisco, eight hundred delegates realizing that court victories and
laws alone won't make them first-class citizens. Thurgood Marshall,
head of the NAACP's legal team, said legal work had to go hand in hand
with community action. It was good news. For the first time maybe since
Lincoln, there's hope that the destination is really in sight. And what
with that group down in Alabama—that Martin Luther King's group—
about to bus-boycott the city of Montgomery to its knees, things are
definitely looking up for the Negro in America in 1956.

Fields doesn't give a shit about that. He does, however, notice that
Miss NAACP is going to be crowned next week at the Pasadena Civic
Auditorium. That's sure something he'd like to see. He'll think on that
later, if he remembers.

His favorite part of the paper is the society page, and best of all he
likes *Dot's Dashes*, Dorothea Foster's column that keeps track of anyone
who's anyone going anywhere that's got some there, there along Central
Avenue. She uses short, simple words and sentences that have dots between them. She's easy to read. Let's see, Fred Griffin's having a cocktail
party dinner party, and Condelis Martin and Dr. Edwin Witt are going

to be there; and "Stairway to the Stars" is the theme of the debutante ball for club Les Beaus Dames. "It's really a wonderful world," Dot declares. "Where big things and little things, happy things and sad things, go to make up the lives we lead."

Fields finishes dinner and the paper at the same time. He feels ready for the night. When he gets home, his landlady, Mrs. Terrell, is out back burning two days' worth of trash in the battered incinerator. He can smell it before he sees it. In the summer you can only incinerate before ten in the morning and after four, and since she has to be cleaning house at Mrs. Benjamin's on the west side of town by seven, Fields puts up with the thick black smoke that pours from the chimney and gets blown by a breeze into his open, unscreened window.

He climbs the stairs to his room, lights a cigarette, and leans out to watch as she tries slamming the big metal door shut. In a year, incinerating trash is going to be illegal. You'll have to put it all in cans and pay more to have it picked up. Mrs. Terrell once told him she thought all the talk about how the new law will clean up L.A.'s air is hot air, that it's only a plot to put more money in the city's pockets. She got the money to buy this place when her Buick was hit by a white man racing through a light and she hired a good Jew lawyer who persuaded two white witnesses to tell the truth.

Fields showers, pours himself a tumbler of Scoresby scotch, turns on the twenty-one-inch Muntz "movable" TV that he paid $79.95 for and just saw in a window for ten bucks less, waiting on it to come on before sitting down so he doesn't have to stand again to change channels to something he likes. *The Adventures of Rin Tin Tin* is on. He likes Rin Tin Tin. But the picture's lousy. He futzes with the rabbit ears and horizontal hold, sits in his chair, and the last thing he sees before dozing off is a commercial for something new called a Swanson TV dinner. If he had an oven instead of just a hot plate, he could make one of those. They look good.

Waking with a start just before nine, Fields catches the last few minutes of *The Adventures of Ozzie & Harriet,* and the happy family ending reminds him that his thirty-fourth birthday is coming up on Sunday. He starts to feel lonesome and might even like to see either the wife or kid he walked out on.

But first things first.

The music's good and the vibe's good and the chances look good at Club Oasis, in the Le Caribe Lounge of the Clark Hotel on Washington and Central. Betty Ann Bryant's at the keyboard, Boots and Vickie are singing, and the place is full of young talent, but none of them is interested in buying what Willie Roscoe Fields is selling tonight. Sometimes it's like that. He walks down the street to the Key Hole Lounge, where the Nat Walker Trio is on the verge of being on *The Steve Allen Show* and maybe stardom, and mixmaster Jimmie Gibson pours drinks that some people swear work like Spanish flies. Not tonight, though. Both places he ends up drinking mostly alone and walking out the door by himself, the girls liking the way he looks but not the way he talks about one thing and one thing only, as if that's all there is; and even if it is all there is, they still want to pretend to talk about something that isn't it, and he can't seem to get through two sentences about the weather or the Rams or the ice cubes in his bourbon without smiling and whispering something about what he can offer between the sheets. So he tries Dynamite Jackson's, the Ambassador Motel, and even Eddie Atkinson's Town Tavern. He has better luck in those places; some nice-looking women blow mentholated smoke rings and drink what he buys them. But that's as far as it goes, and by last call he's drunk and horny and frustrated enough to fuck his DeSoto's gas tank. He needs a lady, and he needs her fast, and he might even have to pay for it, though that offends him on principle.

Willie Fields wonders if he's lost his mojo. He's had a dry spell for weeks now and can't figure it out. All those women, and none of them going home with him. What's changed? He remembers how his wife Ruby loved to love him, and it makes him smile—but only for a second, because memories are no substitute for the real thing unless you're alone in bed in the middle of the night and can't sleep with that big bone daddy that won't go away on its own, and the memories help you get yourself off. Driving, he pats his crotch, like he's comforting it. On the way home, he'll go a little out of his way—one last cruise for some fine lady, even not so fine, who might've had a fight with her boyfriend and jumped out of the car to walk home all pissed off. He detours west, way west, into a part of town the cops don't like seeing his kind at this hour. He'll have to have a story if he gets stopped, tell them he's coming from work. They probably wouldn't believe him anyway, but at least when your story's right there on your tongue, you've got a shot at pulling it off. He thinks hard about it and finally settles on *Good evening, Officer. Where'm I going? I going home after an emergency call from my employer, Mr. White, who lives in Beverly Hills and needed me to come quick fix his toilet. It was runnin' and runnin' and wouldn't stop, and, oh, what a mess. So I got out of bed and drove there at this hour and fixed it up in a jiffy. Drinking? No, I haven't been drinking, 'cept if you count that one shot me and Mr. White had in his kitchen after I finished up to say thank-you. He do that sometimes, Mr. White.*

Where he is now, it's ugly if it's anything at all. But not a mile north is Hancock Park, an area of huge homes with half-acre lawns that slope gracefully to the street. Off Ardmore, just to the south, is a good place for teenagers to park and make out. He knows that, and so do the cops. Sometimes, strictly for fun, they go and put the fear of Parker into them, threatening to arrest the kids on a "morals charge" and call their parents. The girls especially freak out at the thought of dad hearing his little girl's been doing the dirty with that piece of shit who was so polite when he picked her up at seven, promising to have her home by midnight but instead taking her to this dirt lot fifty yards from the closest streetlight where couples neck or better, some of them closing the deal after four hot-and-bothered hours of a double feature at the Gilmore Drive-In The-ater, where there were too many people around to do it without someone

possibly seeing, that someone possibly being the guy across the aisle in
Mr. Hodson's biology class.

Fields slows and sees a blue-and-white '55 Chevy Bel Air. Inside is
a girl, her blond or brown ponytail swinging, next to a broad-shouldered
guy with a flattop, both of them silhouetted by the glow from a long
flashlight that a cop slaps menacingly in his hand while leaning through
the driver's open window, his car parked behind them on the street.
The kids look like they're pleading, bargaining, swearing to God they'll
never again do anything like this, Mr. Policeman. Fields laughs and
speeds up a little so the cop won't see him. He better get home.

Tommy's is on his way, up Venice to Vermont. Toe Main Tommy's—
that's how he thinks you spell the nickname people gave it. If he can't
do the thing with some stone fox, he can at least have some chili dogs
with the fixings. He parks and a guy approaches, a guy as big as he is but
smiling wide.

"Say, brother, 'xcuse me, but I need a hand," the guy says.

"For what?" Fields says.

The guy points half a block up, toward a Nash Rambler, yellow,
ugly—an Earl Scheib job. The Bondo it covers probably cost more than
the paint. "Need a push to jump 'er."

"First let me get somethin' to eat," Fields says.

"Tell you what," the guy says, "you help me, I'll give you a buck.
That'll buy a whole lot of the shit they shovelin' here." Fields doesn't
move. "C'mon, won't take but a minute. Be a Good Samaritan."

"Okay," Fields says.

He walks up the block with the guy. "Terrible what happened to Nat
Cole, ain't it?" the guy says.

"What happened?" Fields asks.

"You didn't hear?"

"Hear what?"

"Man, it was big news."

Nat King Cole was playing the first of two shows in the Birmingham Municipal Auditorium. This being Alabama, it was for whites only—the blacks-only show to start three hours later—and every seat was sold. Cole was backed onstage with white musicians, the first time that had ever happened there, so a sheer curtain had to separate them from where he sat at the piano. In the middle of his third song, "Little Girl," three white men rushed the stage. Two of them tackled him, hurt his back, sent him to the doctor. Show canceled.

"So what happened?" Fields asks.

"Never mind," the guy says. "Not important."

He climbs in his driver's seat, turns the key, depresses the clutch. "All right," he shouts. Fields pushes below the taillights and the car glides away from the curb, gathering steam as Fields hits a trot. The guy shouts, "Good," Fields lets go, the guy pops the clutch, the Nash Rambler sputters alive. The guy guns it till the engine purrs, then he stops, puts the car in neutral, and, when Fields catches up, stands with a revolver in his hand, aimed at Fields.

"Thank you for the push, my brother. Now if you could just, uh, loan me whatever you got in your pocket, I'll have some gasoline money to get home to Frisco."

Fields stares at the gun, as if admiring it, not really focused until the guy lowers his aim to below the waist. "Swear to God, brother," he says, "I'll shoot your dick off. The whole fucking thing."

Fields has about seven bucks left, all in ones. The guy carefully takes them, tells Fields to step back, gets in the car, and drops a dollar bill on the street. "Enjoy your meal," he says before speeding away and hanging a right on Venice.

There's nothing to see anymore, not even to hear, but Fields can't stop staring at the place where this happened. He's still thinking, still thinking, still thinking. And now he's done thinking.

CHAPTER FIVE

Danny Galindo stands on the corner of East First Street and Alameda, not far from the downtown Police Administration Building. He glances up at the sign for the Christmas Hotel, which he just learned from talking to the guy is named for Leonard Christmas. Danny doesn't know if that's his real name.

Earlier that morning Christmas peered over room 329's transom and saw the two bodies. On the bed, partially covered by a sheet, was Gijou T. David, three gaping gunshot wounds in his belly and chest. On the floor next to the bed was Wardell Holman, a hole in his right temple to match the .32 pistol lying near his open hand, his naked corpse blocking the door. The cops had to break through the window and move the body's legs before opening the door. Danny got there just before the coroner and confirmed the powder burns on Holman's hand and forehead, leaving murder-suicide as the only justifiable conclusion. Nothing else in the room suggests a third party, and the only thing that bothered Danny, confirmed with the coroner, was how long it took David to die. Judging by the amount of blood, his heart kept pumping a while, maybe hours, so what Danny wants to know now from Miss Cecil Lloyd, who lives in the next room, was what she heard and when.

"It was 'bout seven thirty," she says. "They was arguin'."

"About what?"

"I don't know."

"You don't know, or you won't say?" He can see her hesitancy. She's embarrassed. No need to press why.

She looks down. That's her answer.

"All right, then what did you hear?" he asks.

"Gunshots." she says.

"You're sure? You know the sound of gunfire?"

Now she looks at him like this must be his first day off the bus. "Yes, sir, I do," she says, a little disgust in her tone.

"Well then, Miss Lloyd," Danny says, "if you're familiar with what a gun sounds like, and you hear it at least four times, and then the voices that you've heard before suddenly stop, how come you never called the cops? Or anybody? If you had, one of those men might be alive."

Now she's got nothing to say. Neither does he.

He looks up one last time at the decaying Christmas Hotel sign and wonders if Christmas will ever be the same.

CHAPTER SIX

There are homes in Los Angeles the size of small fiefdoms, grand homes with acres of lush grounds manicured by Japanese gardeners who may have once worked for Emperor Hirohito. These are homes you reach at the end of driveways that resemble country lanes bordered on both sides by trees that form a lush canopy; homes whose front doors are too far from the street to reach by foot; homes built for men with fortunes that came from real estate, oil, citrus, transportation, war factories, movies, or water; men whose names would be lost to history except for the hundreds of eponymous streets on which millions now live in homes built by other of these men; men whose descendants enjoy lives of privilege and luxury bought by three generations of satisfied wants—descendants whose occasional debauchery comes from never having had to satisfy such wants through the sweat of their own brow.

Sometimes people get hurt or worse in these homes. Sometimes people turn up dead there, or don't turn up at all, or their jewels go missing, and sometimes something comes to someone's attention. Then there's no alternative but to get the police involved, even if they don't want to, and they rarely do unless there's already a certain understanding in place with the DA. When that happens, no captain or lieutenant is going to send a brown-skinned detective in to make things right with Mr. Money or Mrs. Power.

Only handpicked detectives, like Thad Brown, are allowed inside when someone in them happens to die unusually or kill unusually or is raped and robbed by an intruder who manages to evade security, or after the dope fiend scion of another prominent family falls into the pool.

Matter of fact, Chief of Detectives Brown has taken the lead on a case in Bel Air, where few crimes occur, but when they do, they sell newspapers. Evelyn Scott, the wealthy wife of one L. Ewing Scott, hasn't been seen in over a year. She's no doubt dead, and Scott, the only one of Evelyn's five husbands not to have his own money, no doubt did it and ditched the body—or pieces of it—somewhere good. What complicated the investigation was that Evelyn's brother had been living abroad, so it took him ten months to report his sister missing from her own home. By then the only evidence a two-day search turned up in the dirt six inches beneath thick foliage outside that Bel Air mansion were her dentures and eyeglasses; and in the incinerator ashes were the remains of some hosiery fasteners. How do you prosecute a murder without a body? Scott claimed his wife had gone out for a pack of cigarettes and kept going, that she was on a long bender with her lesbian lover. By the time Brown and the DA got involved, the best they were able to do was charge Scott with forgery and fraud for looting his wife's bank accounts and safe-deposit boxes. He posted the bail and took off, and after a national manhunt everyone in Homicide is sure he's in either Mexico or Canada, living the good life on wads of cash. Danny bets Canada because Mexico's too obvious, and a guy who could make a body disappear and sanitize the car of evidence is too clever to do the obvious. Besides, the fact that Scott hides his first name, thinking that L. Ewing

Scott sounds more refined than Leonard, means there's no way he's hanging out with Mexes, not even in Acapulco.

Homes like Evelyn Scott's aren't the kind that Danny Galindo is assigned to visit. Sure, he'd like to see behind those gates, if only to satisfy his curiosity, and he believes he will someday. Maybe not in five years, but possibly in ten, definitely no more than fifteen. And if he never gets there, that's all right, too. He'll always respect the honest crooks with a gun (unless they pull the trigger) more than he does the swells who're born to it yet still take more by telling the gullible what they want to hear about how pretty or talented they are. The rich know that people with nothing think people with everything can be talked into giving them anything.

Danny was twenty-five when he ended up back in L.A. after the war, wondering what to do with himself. A white probation officer who spent a lot of time in the barrio looking for that jewel in the rough found one on a rainy night when he ran out of gas and Danny came to his aid. The PO could see how smart Danny was and asked what he wanted out of life. Danny told him more than this, the guy said the LAPD was a good place to be, and Danny said that sounded fine. The guy wrote a recommendation to the academy and made sure Danny had the dough to get him through. A year later poor Elizabeth Short's bad end was as much Danny's ticket out of patrol as his logical brain and cool temperament. Whatever happened after that would be up to him.

Being from the street is what makes Danny a good detective. He wonders if it's even possible for a rich kid to do what he does as well as he does it. The kid would have to have stolen from his mom's purse and his father's wallet, gotten away with it, and learned to suspect that everyone he knew was using him for his pool and his parties and his Rams tickets and his grandstand seats at the Rose Parade. Even so, being cynical isn't the same as being skeptical. Cynics always inject themselves into the story, which makes it hard to get a good read on the facts.

No, for this kind of work, the law of the jungle is the best preparation. Danny has read plenty of Sherlock Holmes, and he doubts that the wizard of Baker Street would wrap things up quite so neatly or easily in 1950s Los Angeles, where the kind of crime and quality of criminal would mean getting his hands dirty. Holmes may have more pure smarts than he does, but Danny's pretty sure that the great detective would've gotten the shit knocked out of him every day after school on the mean streets of El Paso and then the meaner streets of Boyle Heights, L.A.; wouldn't have showed the guts to enlist in the war; wouldn't have survived getting shot down by German artillery fire; wouldn't have plotted an escape from the POW camp; couldn't have endured the rigors of the escape itself, and the days and then weeks of hiding on the run, scrounging like a dog, and finally making it back to the safety of an American unit; wouldn't have immediately volunteered for more missions—and would've then lost faith after being shot down a second time and spending the rest of the war in a four-sided concrete room. Sherlock Holmes didn't do that. Danny did. Sherlock Holmes isn't real. Danny's real.

He's at the Olympic Auditorium on Grand Avenue downtown. It smells of stale beer, sweat, and popcorn. A wonderful place, the crossroads of L.A. He likes it better than Wrigley Field, where the Angels baseball team plays. Danny was here the previous night, too, to watch wrestling. He loves Bobo Brazil, a six-six black man—wrestling's Jackie Robinson—with a voice soft as harp strings but whose best move is smashing his forehead into his opponent's, something he calls the "coco butt." Danny knows it's fake, but no less fake than the ballet or theater and a lot more entertaining. Nearly every one of his informants comes here, whether for wrestling, Roller Derby, or boxing. Tonight's boxing, strictly on the level. Or at least it's supposed to be. So the clientele's a little different. They behave better until the blood spurts from the ring or the ref and judges do something that looks like maybe some money passed hands.

The main event is Kid Gavilan against Ramon Fuentes, welterweights, Gavilan the bolo-punching former champ with 105 wins, now ranked eighth and an L.A. darling, the Olympic his favorite venue. Born Gerardo Gonzáles in Havana, the "Cuban Hawk" is 6 to 5 in the betting, having looked sharper in whipping Chico Vejar than Fuentes did, and Gavilan already beat Fuentes once in a unanimous decision three years ago in Milwaukee, where they're supposed to know good fighters, especially if one of them's German. Danny doesn't care who wins, though he and Gavilan go way back, and if he wins, Gavilan will be matched against Art Aragon, another L.A. kid made good. Really good. Good enough to have just been in a movie with Audie Murphy.

Besides rooting for friends, Danny just likes being here, among the action. Everyone in the place could've stayed home to watch the bouts on Channel 5. But they came for the same reason that folks spend a lot more money to drink at a bar than they would out of a bottle alone at home. Except for the bottle, the same goes for him, by the way. Living alone is hard, even when you think it's better than the alternative; even when your guests stay till morning.

Anyway, you never know what you're going to find out or see here. Maybe a hundred of the people in the cheap seats have rap sheets, some with Danny's name on it. The guy at the door knows to let Danny in. Aileen Eaton, the promoter, appreciates having as many cops there as possible. Some nights it's like a cop bar, and the more the riffraff gets that, the less chance there is some asshole will try to pull something on someone he thinks is a civilian.

The last undercard bout has just finished, Mickey Northrup against Rudy Jordan. Judging by the buzz, Danny didn't miss anything. He strolls the floor, scanning the crowd. He can't help himself. Sometimes he thinks he should put in for eighteen hours of overtime a day. Even when he's asleep, he's working angles on cases. It doesn't matter that so many people recognize him. It's good that they do. He's not an undercover dick, he's a plainclothes detective, a shield in his belt and a revolver in his shoulder holster. Besides, everyone who recognizes him recognizes him for a reason.

There's Eddie Dunne, the little twerp he popped four years ago. The guy used to read the newspaper obituaries, which print the deceased's home address, then show up during the scheduled funeral time, which was also printed, and clean the place out, knowing no one was home. Scum. Normally, Danny wouldn't have taken a burglary, but he'd happened to read the beat cop's report (as he loves doing off-hours) of a twenty-five-year-old widow, mother of a two-year-old girl, her thirty-year-old husband, a jeweler, having just died of cancer. When she came back to her apartment, she saw her clothing on the floor and every piece of furniture—and every gem from her husband's work—gone. Eddie and his crew, wearing overalls, had brazenly backed a truck up to the door and carried out their heist with smiles for the neighbors, who figured poor Mrs. Bryman was moving now. She was left with nothing for herself or the kid, and the report said she was weeping so hard the cop was afraid to leave her alone.

Enraged, Danny hoarded this case (not that anyone else wanted it). He called other divisions to see how many like crimes there'd been, and of course Eddie wasn't the only piece of garbage who could read the papers; for years cops had been trying to get the obituary writers to omit addresses, but it was standard news style to include everyone's address, criminals and their victims, the living and the dead—and anyway, editors argued, city directories and phone books both contained everyone's address.

What made Eddie's MO unique was its brazenness. Funeral thieves usually break in a back door and search for valuables, then slip out, and you can usually find some of their stuff at pawnshops. Not Eddie. In the previous few months four homes in four divisions had been hit the same way. Which meant some thoughtful deliberation was going on. The key was to figure out what the criteria were and then watch the obits. It took weeks before Danny read about another young widow, her late husband a professional, neither of them originally from L.A., so they'd have no family. Danny was waiting inside when Eddie's van got there, and now Danny makes sure that Eddie sees him standing in the aisle. The time at Folsom seems not to have agreed with Eddie, who was a two-time loser before then. Neither does seeing the man who put him there.

"Hiya, Eddie," Danny says.

Eddie's lips say nothing but after he absorbs the surprise his eyes glare a fuck-you at Danny. "Detective Galindo," he finally manages.

"C'mon, Eddie, lighten up," Danny says. "You know I could bust your parole right now if I wanted."

"Yeah, how's that?"

"Consorting with known felons."

"Bullshit. Who?"

Danny points at two men sitting within a few rows of Danny, both with convictions for far worse and more violent crimes than Eddie's. "That's Lou Morgan," Danny says, "a dope dealer turned armed robber. And there's Rodney Carlton. Cut his own brother for some cigarettes."

Eddie's a nothing. But maybe because he preyed on the most vulnerable, the creep holds a special place in Danny's pantheon of justice. It's a hell of a lot of fun to yank the guy's chain.

"Maybe you know them," Danny says.

"No," Eddie insists. "Never met."

Danny smiles. "Enjoy the fight."

Ten minutes to the big event. Danny's welcome in Gavilan's dressing room, if he wants, to wish the man luck. But instead he'll just find an unsold seat somewhere. On the way, he laughs. That Oldsmobile dealer, Yeakel, who advertises on TV, is taking a ribbing from some friends. A week ago, ad-libbing during a live ad, as these guys do, the words "nigger in the woodpile" popped out. Half an hour later, the local NAACP secretary called up, and since then half the Negroes in L.A. have asked whether they might get themselves an apology deal. The blowhard hasn't stopped explaining that he has no idea how that phrase, "which I never ever use," happened to slip. It'll all blow over. What're they going to do, boycott him? Yeah, right. In fact, Yeakel might get himself more cops for customers now.

Danny takes a seat on an aisle near the back. If someone comes to claim it, he'll move over.

It's a good fight, goes all ten rounds, the crowd on its feet much of the time until a split decision gives Fuentes his thirty-ninth win and Gavilan his twenty-third loss. Danny would've called it a draw. He can see that neither fighter has more than a year or two left unless he's paired with some tomato cans out in the sticks where they don't know any better.

Now's not a good time to go back and see Gavilan. Which means Danny has to go home. He'll take the long way. And get there too soon.

CHAPTER SEVEN

BLIND VET BEATEN BY POLICE

Two policemen were accused of violently beating a blinded veteran of World War II while he was walking to his car and of forcing his wife who had broken her ankle months earlier to walk without her crutches while her hands were cuffed behind her back.

Wilson White, 709 E. 33rd Pl., who despite his handicap has been a worker at Hughes Aircraft Company for the past five years, claimed that police dragged him from his car as he was leaving the American Legion Hall, 1312 W. 3rd St., about one a.m. Saturday morning, where he and his wife Sally had attended an affair given by the Blinded Veterans Association.

A number of people who witnessed the event shouted to police that the man was blind but to no avail.

Mrs. White, meanwhile, had gotten out of the car and pleaded with the officers not to beat her husband. She was on crutches, since one of her ankles had been broken and was in a cast. One of the policeman turned to her and forced her arms behind her back and handcuffed her. With her hands pinned in back of her, she could not use the crutches. The officer took them from her and forced her to hobble as best she could.

White formally served with the Buffalo Division of the 92nd Infantry, which was stationed in Italy in 1944. He was blinded in both eyes and suffered an injury to the right ear when a land-mine exploded. He has lived in Los Angeles since 1936 and owns his own home.

—An article that appeared in the *California Eagle* but not in any white newspaper— not the *Los Angeles Times,* the *Herald-Express,* the *Examiner,* the *Mirror*—during the summer of 1956.

CHAPTER EIGHT

It's Saturday. Willie Fields spends part of it at the Army-Navy Surplus Store on Santa Monica Boulevard, in Hollywood. Some of the stuff there he remembers seeing before getting thrown in the stockade. He buys a twelve-inch flashlight that uses D, silver Eveready batteries stacked in the handle. Forget the light it puts off, the thing's a lethal weapon.

Around the corner is a J.J. Newberry's. He wanders up and down aisles until he finds what he wants: a tin sheriff's badge.

In the car, he takes the contents of both bags and hides them in the glove box. On the way home he turns on the radio. Half a minute passes before he hears, "We're gonna be goin' strong till two o'clock this morning. So if you're cruisin' around in the Rocket 88, keep it tuned right here to KPOP for any jumpin' little records you want your DJ to play." And now Chuck Berry is singing "Roll Over, Beethoven." "Gonna write a little letter, gonna mail it to my local DJ. Yeah, and it's a jumpin' little record I want my jockey to play . . ."

Fields keeps time with his head and twice glances over at the closed glove box. He feels right with the world.

The song ends and now the man speaks again. "Good huntin' with Hunter. This is Hunter Hancock, ol' H.H. on the fabulous KPOP, your home for rhythm and blues. We got the rhythm so you don't get the blues. The greatest entertainers in the world, brought to you by Bibb's Department Store, Royal Crown Cola, and Dolphin's of Hollywood Records, where you can buy everything you hear here and much more. Come on down to Vernon and Central and meet John Dolphin himself, the man who knows what's selling where and to who. And here's one that's really selling for the Platters"—who sing "You've Got the Magic Touch." Fields sings along, "*I've* got the magic touch . . . ," in a voice that might not get him a job with the Platters but wouldn't get him laughed off the stage, either. All those years of church choir.

He heads south on Highland, liking being in Hancock Park, where the brick homes are set back from the street, separated by those huge lawns. Then he turns east on Wilshire to Crenshaw, south to Olympic, and east again the five miles or so till Central. With every block the streets and air and scenery and cars get dirtier and uglier.

Outside Dolphin's of Hollywood Records—which isn't in Hollywood, so Fields always wonders about that—is a line, and it's a line of at least half white kids. Teenagers. Blond girls with ponytails, some in poodle skirts, white boys wearing white T-shirts rolled at their biceps and cuffed blue jeans, their hair pomaded back into duck asses. He has to park two blocks away and gets close enough to the store to peek in and see a poster in the window that says 78S AND 45S ARE 69 CENTS EACH TODAY ONLY below another poster that says LITTLE RICHARD, APPEARING TONIGHT AT THE SAVOY BALLROOM with a picture of the man—and good golly, there's the man himself, right there, in the flesh, just like anyone else, signing away and looking pleased to be there.

Fields stares at him long enough to get bored, then walks down to Johnny's Grill for a burger, sitting on one of the three red stools at the counter window along Central where you watch Johnny working the griddle. He asks Johnny what's doing with all the white kids, and Johnny says ever since that Elvis Presley, "That's us they playin' on the radio. They calling rhythm 'n' blues rock 'n' roll. You see the commotion at the airport when that boy landed last year? Almost a riot. Thousands of kids, white and black, girls fainting. Look how they showin' up like that for a Negro—Little Richie. 'Bout a year now, half the kids in Dolphin are white."

"I never noticed," Fields says.

"Well, they not usually out the door. And they gone by dark."

Fields laughs. "I know where they goin'—poon city."

Johnny gives him a look like *What the hell's that mean?*

Walking to his DeSoto, Fields sees a yellow car crossing Vernon on Wadsworth. Maybe it's the car that belongs to the guy who rolled him. He hurries the rest of the way to the parking spot, jumps in, has to wait for the big yellow electric streetcar—the S line—to pass before he can pull into traffic. He turns right on East Forty-third Place, weaving through cars to chase one that's nowhere ahead. So he speeds on to Compton Avenue, turns up to East Forty-first, over to Alameda, down to Fiftieth, then makes a U-turn and heads back west, knowing that even if he finds the car, it'll only be by accident, and anyway, it probably won't be the Nash Rambler. But he's got nothing but time to kill till late. He might as well try looking for that mofo who rolled him. Finding him will be just a cherry on top of whatever he's eating tonight.

On Forty-second Place at Avalon, Fields passes Wrigley Field, the stadium where the Angels play. They're pretty good this year. They got this big guy named Bilko who hits a lot of homers. Or wait, maybe Bilko is the name of that funny guy on TV, the one with glasses, in the army. Anyway, the place looks empty, no cars, no people. The team must not be in town. Maybe he'll go to a game this season. Last week he walked over, paid a buck, watched Sugar Ray Robinson fight Bobo Olson in front of twenty thousand for the championship. They put the ring right around home plate and a bunch of seats on the field. He sat in the upper level but his eyes are good so he could see okay. Not that there was much to see. For the first three rounds the fighters looked as if they were dancing, and people booed. Then Robinson hit Olson with a left and that was that. Sugar Ray was champ again. The people went crazy, standing and cheering and clapping and whistling—for a black guy against a white guy. Fields noticed that.

He circles the stadium three times before peeling off and driving around aimlessly till ten, about two hours after forgetting that he's supposed to be looking for a car, not fine women. He goes home, showers, has a drink, then another, and dresses in gabardine slacks—or at least something that's supposed to pass for gabardine—and a pressed cotton shirt. He slips on a light sport coat and pulls something from one of his dresser's three drawers. It's a switchblade, which he flicks open and tests with his wrist, cutting the air right to left and left to right, before closing the blade and putting it in his jacket pocket. He checks himself in the mirror.

It's too late to see Little Richard, and he can't get into the late show at Zardi's Jazzland, to see Shelly Manne, so he stops at the Chez Paree Lounge, where Dudley Brook is still quietly at the piano, playing what makes people look better to each other. He has a couple of drinks and tries to get loose. Only, his heart's not in it tonight. No one interests him. No one's interested in him. Same result at Club Milomo.

Half past midnight he drives west and north, to a part of town he'd driven through earlier on the way back from Hollywood, a place he better not be seen by a cop this time of night. He tries to remember that story he made up about Mr. White's toilet in Beverly Hills. *What if they ask what street he lives on? Yeah, sure, Beverly Hills Boulevard. Better make it Avenue. Or, wait, Street. No, Avenue.*

Around Highland and San Vicente, away from the busy corner, is a lookout where kids go in their parents' cars. He knew it was there to be found because there's always one near a high school, in this case L.A. High, but more important a country club—in this case, Wilshire Country Club, five minutes north. Willie Roscoe Fields is familiar with the mating habits of young Americans.

The lot is hosting two cars, about thirty yards apart, and at this hour there's likely to be some serious action going on. He parks on the street, takes the flashlight and badge from his glove box, and sneaks behind the closest car, a new Ford Ranch Wagon. The windows are steamed up, so he can't see inside. He figures they're in back and raps lightly on the driver's window with the flashlight, which freaks the hell out of the kids inside. He hears shrieks and then a hand from inside wipes a porthole and the boy sees Fields's face. They're in the front seat—and look like they're going to crap. Fields flashes the badge and motions to roll down the window. The boy cranks it open. He's not more than sixteen, and so's his girlfriend, who might actually be fifteen. They hadn't gotten past second base and maybe weren't planning on it—or at least she may not have been—because Fields can see her bra's still intact beneath her top two unbuttoned buttons that she's quickly buttoning.

"Undercover vice squad," Fields says. This is going to be easy. "Get out the car."

The other car must've heard or seen something. It starts up and drives off. "Come on," Fields says. "Out. Both of you."

The girl is pretty. Brown hair. He's going to show her something she's never seen.

"You committing a morals charge?" Fields asks.

"No, sir," the boy says, his voice shaky.

"Do you promise?" Fields says.

"Promise? Yes, I promise," the boy says. "I promise. Really."

"Good. Now here's what you're gonna do. You're gonna get in this car and roll up the windows and sit here like a good boy while I run a check on her. If everything checks out, I'll bring her back and you take her home."

The boy looks over at the girl. "Get over here, young lady," Fields says. Then to the boy: "G'wan."

The boy climbs in the car and rolls up the window as Fields grabs the girl's upper arm and leads her to his car. She sniffles, holding back the tears as much as possible. "Ain't nothin' to worry 'bout," Fields says, "long as you check out."

He opens the door and without protest she gets in the passenger's seat, maybe because she thinks he's really a cop and maybe because, even if he's not, there's no point resisting, but more likely because she's young and has no reason to disbelieve him.

"How old are you?" he asks as they drive. He cuts over to Sixth Street, parallel to Wilshire. It's darker, less busy, more unlikely a cop will see a black man driving with a white teenage girl.

"Where we going?" she asks.

"To the station, so I can check you out. How old are you?"

"Sixteen," she says. "Wanna see my license?"

"When we get there. Why you out with your boyfriend so late?"

"We weren't doin' anything," she says.

"I seen you with my own eyes," he says.

"Kissing, that's all."

"Whose car is that?"

"His mom's."

"Your parents know where you are?"

"I don't know," she says, then reluctantly, "No. But I'm a good girl. Please. I'm waiting till marriage."

Her fear turns him on, and he doesn't need any help.

He cuts down to Eighth Street, then turns east a bit before picking out a dark corner. He stops, parks, turns off the engine and lights, looks over at her, smiles—like they've both been anticipating this moment. Now she knows what's about to happen, and before she can scream, he slaps a hand over her mouth, and before she knows it they're in the back-seat. "Ain't no use fussin'," he says, "you're gonna be braggin' to all your friends come the start of school." And he believes that. He truly does.

She goes somewhere else in her mind while it's happening, and there is nothing inherently violent about what's happening other than this is a man who, if God really watched out for and protected his innocent crea-tures, would never have been there stealing her soul, her dreams, her virginity, and her sanity, all the while talking about how good she feels to him and telling her to tell him the same before his final shuddering grunt, after which he sighs with satisfaction and lights a cigarette.

But this is not that universe. And God is nowhere to be found on this night. And when Fields drops her off half a block from the car where her former boyfriend still waits as he'd been told, the rapist acts as though this had been their first date, a good one, one worthy of a second—and a good-night kiss.

"Thank you," he says softly, leaning over and opening the door for her as this weeping puddle of a girl, who feels him leaking out of her, nearly falls from the car before he speeds away.

Claude's Dogs, better than Toe Main Tommy's, is on the way home. He's hungry. He stands at the outside counter, enjoying his burger and the glow of having just made love. A few months from now, if you told him that this young girl had killed herself, he would've shaken his head and wondered what in the world would drive such a sweet young thing with her whole life ahead of her to do something like that.

CHAPTER NINE

As rapes go, it was ugly. And Danny is having a hard time getting additional details out of the victim, Miss Annette V. Evans. She's pretty, single, black, thirty-two, a Sunday-school teacher from Atlanta who, a week ago today, took the train across country for the National Baptist Sunday School and Training Union Congress, held this year in L.A., at Carver Junior High. South of Vernon Avenue is a crummy area of town for people who don't know the city—but what are you going to do, hold a convention of black Baptists in Beverly Hills? Danny reads the black papers, the *Eagle* and *Sentinel*. He knew the delegates were coming— ten thousand of them—and so did the scum who raped her. Or maybe it was a crime of opportunity. Either way, it's yet another confirmation that believing in God doesn't necessarily mean God believes in you.

What Miss Evans has managed to say so far is that she saw three young men in the school's hallway and, assuming that they were also Baptist delegates attending the same class she was headed to, followed them up the stairs to an otherwise deserted wing of the second floor. She didn't realize it was deserted, though, until she walked behind one of them into room 217. Seeing the empty seats, she turned to flee. Too late; the others had closed in behind. One of them held an X-Acto knife to her throat and asked, "Are you afraid?" She nodded yes and begged them not to kill her, promising to do anything they wanted if they'd spare her life. *Anything.* They pushed her down onto the floor and did anything they wanted, and when they were finished they stole her wallet and camera and ordered her to keep quiet for ten minutes.

It's now been three hours.

"Did you hear any of them call the others by name?" Danny asks.

"No," she says sadly.

"We'll find them," Danny assures her, looking professional but showing enough empathy to let her know he takes this personally.

She hasn't been to the hospital yet. No one has even suggested it. Desk sergeant Lorraine Olson had been the first person Annette talked to when she walked in alongside a senior member of the Baptist convention, and Olson had been less than polite. Whatever compassion she might have felt for the young woman—and there's no guarantee she had any at all—would've been overpowered by her outrage over those rampaging nigger hoodlums, or words to that effect, none of them alien to her vocabulary. She doesn't even like black cops. Or so she pretends. Danny took a psychology course at L.A. City College after auditing some criminology classes before being made detective and suspects that Lorraine actually had a crush on his old friend Todd Roark, the cop who supposedly got axed for kiting a check when really it was because he dated white women—white women, that is, who weren't Lorraine Olson. If Danny's right, and he's far from sure, that must've really chapped her. What other reason does she have to still keep Todd's academy photo in her desk? Danny's seen it.

Would he have been assigned this case if the victim were white? He doesn't know. He does know that if a white woman had been gang-raped by three black men, half the department would've been out there with brass knuckles.

"I have to go back to Atlanta," Annette says. It's more shame than stoic bravery. Danny notices her hand shaking.

"I prefer not to ask you directly," he says, "but I'd like you to extend your stay another few days. I understand that the convention will pay your expenses here and for you to fly home instead of taking the train." He glances up at the elderly lady who brought Annette to the station.

The lady nods while putting her hands gently on Annette's shoulders.

"I've never been on a plane," Annette says.

"If we find them soon, and I think we will," Danny says, "you might get back around the same time that you would've if you took the train. Maybe a day or two more total." He thinks they're local guys who had to have walked in the front door, will be bragging about what they did in the neighborhood, and will either look stupid taking pictures with the camera or act stupid by trying to sell it.

"Why do I have to stay?"

"You're the only person who could identify them. If you're not here, we'd have to let them go"—after first knocking the shit out of them.

"Then do I have to come back after that?"

"Not if there's not a trial," Danny explains. "They may cop a plea if their attorney thinks they'll lose in court, and they will. If they don't, well—you'll have to testify."

"I don't know if I can do that."

"You can," he insists. "And you have to. Because if we don't get these animals off the street, they'll keep doing this to other women. Possibly they've done this to other women who refused for one reason or another to come forward, and that's why it happened to you."

The old lady puts her hand on Annette's shoulder again as a buoy. Annette looks at her, then at Danny. She nods. This has just become her Christian duty. Danny can see that. Now she's Job. She's Jesus on

Calvary. She's not being given a burden heavier than God knows she can carry.

"Okay," she says.

"Good," he says. He wants to show her some photos of known rapists, but first he's bringing in the sketch artist. Once the drawings are done, he's going to take her in another room and show her the photos. If she picks any, he'll compare them to the drawings. That will tell him a lot about her reliability and what kind of witness she'll make. Then she can go to the hospital. If she wants.

CHAPTER TEN

The corner of Valencia and Ingraham forms a T where Ingraham begins and Valencia dead-ends into an open field abutting this underdeveloped neighborhood just west of downtown L.A. There's a nice view of twinkling lights to the west and the north, and at this hour half a dozen cars are parked with lovers inside. Some are still in foreplay, some in the hump stage, some already primping for the ride home and letting the fog air out, maybe even smoking cigarettes. All of them infuriate him.

Fields picks his target—that old Ford off by itself—and takes the badge and flashlight from his glove compartment. He walks to the driver's window and stares in at the couple. They must not have been in there long because the windows are still clear and the clothes still intact. They're talking. Three raps of the flashlight on the driver's door changes that.

"Get out of the car," he says.

"What the hell?" says the young man. He's white, midtwenties with a military haircut.

Fields steps back two strides, impatiently slapping the flashlight into his left palm. From this angle he can see the young lady, and he realizes he's picked the right car. "Hurry up."

The girl steps out first. Her name's Margaret Bollinger. She's pretty with plump cheeks and doe eyes—everything about her ripe for plucking, Fields decides. Her young man, Charles Barker, carefully slides out from his side, dropping the car keys into his front pocket. He's muscular but not particularly tall and looks a bit older than his date. Both he and Margie will later describe their assailant as a "huge Negro."

Fields lets them study him in silence. He towers over his prey and enjoys his intimidating power. This is a neighborhood in which a huge Negro's unsolicited presence at 1:00 a.m. is rarely good news.

"Sheriff's vice," Fields says, opening his wallet to flash the badge he's stuffed in. When he closes the wallet, Barker says, "May I see that again, sir?" the *sir* added on without even thinking, this being year three of his four-year commitment to the Marines, where *Yes, sir* and *No, sir* are automatic. As they are in Alabama, too, though not for black civilians.

"How come?" Fields asks.

Barker doesn't say so, but from the little he saw, that badge looks like the one he used to have pinned to his cowboy vest when he was five. Besides, how many plainclothes Negro vice cops are there, even in Los Angeles?

"Just want to make sure you are who you say you are?" Barker says nervously.

"Who would I be?" Fields says.

"Anybody, I guess." Barker says.

Fields flashes the badge again, *flash* being the operative word.

"I'm undercover," Fields says. "Vice. You two been committing a morals charge. It's my duty to take you in."

"We weren't doing anything," Margie says. "Honest."

Not yet has Margie learned to mistrust a man's word, whatever the color of his skin or the hour of the morning. Twenty years old, she's been here only a few weeks from rural Washington, apple country, where experiences that might've made her pray for this man to be what he claimed to be happened only in movies. Growing up, she'd always wanted to travel, to see other places, meet new people, especially the big city, and Los Angeles is just the first stop in her master plan that has her ending up somewhere else. She lives in a brick boardinghouse three blocks away on Ingraham, was set up on this blind date by a girl from Iowa who lives down the hall, has just gotten done seeing *Invasion of the Body Snatchers* at the El Rey, and needs to be back within the hour or she'll hear about it in the morning from her landlady, who thinks of the girls in her charge as her kids.

"I saw you with my own eyes," Fields says.

"It was just a ki—"

Barker interrupts her. He says, "I don't believe you're who you say you are."

"What do you mean? I'm a sheriff's deputy. Showed you my badge."

"I don't think so."

Fields stares at him for a moment, looks around, points down the block to a phone booth a hundred yards behind Barker on the dimly lit corner. "Why don't you go right over and call the police station and ax them do they got an officer Thomas Lonnon on the force."

"I thought you said you were a sheriff," Barker says.

"That's right."

"So why would I call the *police* station?" Barker says. Not that he needs any more confirmation, but he can tell by the little stutter in Fields's eyes that this guy's no kind of cop.

"Go ahead," Fields says. "Call. We'll wait here for you."

Now Barker understands. "No," he says.

Maybe on another night, when he's not so turned on that he hopes he doesn't get a hard-on right then and there, Fields might've laughed it off and walked away. But not tonight, not looking at Margie. He's more horny than mad, but that leaves plenty of room for being mad. And a good reason for it.

His right hand inches toward his left shoulder, intimating that there's a weapon under the blue Windbreaker. He wishes he'd brought the switchblade, but he forgot it in the glove box.

"Let's go," he says. "I'm taking you two in to the central jail for lewd conduct. Get in the car." His head motions toward the DeSoto parked on the street.

"In that?" Barker says. "That's your car?"

"Yeah, that's the car.

"Doesn't look like a cop car."

"Not s'pposed to. That there's an undercover car," Fields says, his hand still threatening. "Something wrong with it?"

"A DeSoto?" Barker says. "I thought you'd have a Cadillac or something."

"Yeah?" Fields doesn't know if this guy's playing with him. "Get goin'." He steps aside and motions with his head, like in the movies.

Barker avoids Margie's eyes. He's afraid she might read his thoughts and say something that startles Fields into doing something before Barker's ready for him to do it. Barker already knows what Fields wants. In Alabama, where Barker's from, whites know that Negro men want only one thing, and he knows what they're willing to do for it—or so he's heard. So it's said. So he's been told.

Barker walks behind Margie, Fields behind Barker, toward the DeSoto. Barker wishes the car had been parked on the other side of the street; he'd be able to cross in front or behind and read the license plate. They come up on the passenger side.

Fields opens the door, says, "She sits in back," but Barker snatches Margie by the arm and pushes her in the front seat, in the middle. He sits to her right, shotgun.

"Okay," Fields says, hurrying around to the driver's side.

He gets in and starts up. For the first time, Margie can smell the alcohol on his breath. For the first time, she's afraid. Barker puts his hand on her knee, a way of saying there's nothing to worry about. Fields notices, then realizes that the knife is in the glove box right in front of Barker. Barker leans his hands on the dash, just above the box. Fields wonders whether he's got X-ray vision, like Superman.

"Get your hands off that," Fields says before pulling away.

The DeSoto moves north and west. Fields drives carefully, attracting no attention.

Barker leans forward to stare at him, hands on his knees. What he's really trying to see is the car registration in a clear plastic sleeve affixed to the steering column. He can't read it.

Fields doesn't acknowledge Barker's staring at him except for furtive glances. He keeps his eyes on the street and his right hand under his jacket, moving it only to shift gears on the column. He has to act cool, like a cop doing his job with the law behind him and all the confidence in the world.

Fields can't keep the silence, though. He says, "You kids shouldn't be doin' it in the car."

"My landlady won't let us have visitors," Margie says. "Not even for coffee. She's very strict."

"Um-hmmm," Fields says. "That ain't no excuse."

"Where we going?" Barker asks.

"I'm gonna have to conduct a physical exam on you two before I take you in."

"Like hell," Barker whispers under his breath.

"Huh?" Fields says.

Barker doesn't repeat himself.

The car pulls to a darkened curb. Of the three, only Fields knows that they're a few blocks from the San Pedro Street entrance to the L.A. city jail and LAPD headquarters administration building, where he was booked seven years ago. It's around the corner from where he stood in court, too. There was no reason to get so close to a real cop station. In fact, it was way past stupid. But concentrating so hard on acting like a cop, he forgot himself. He puts the transmission in neutral and lifts his foot off the clutch.

"You sit still, young lady, while I search your gentleman first," he says. "I gotta do that before I get you to the station."

Now Fields meets Barker's gaze. "Get out. On the sidewalk."

"Okay," Barker says.

He opens the door and lets it swing to its apogee and stop before glancing one last time at Fields, who he's sure is waiting to step on that clutch and jam the thing into first.

"Aren't you getting out, too?" Barker asks.

"Course I am. I got to pat you down," Fields says.

"I'm ready," Barker says.

Just like that Barker grabs the crook of Margie's right elbow and yanks, pulling her with him in a motion that lands both of them on the narrow grass median, then onto the sidewalk in a sideways roll. He guides her with one arm to stand behind him. She's as startled as Fields, it all happened so fast.

Barker knows Fields would have driven away with Margie, and he's about to find out whether there really is a gun under that jacket. The Marines have taught him a lot about self-defense and hand-to-hand combat, but this is one fatally large man. He pulls the keys from his pocket and readies for battle, holding his arms out in some kind of pose, turning his fist into a barbed weapon with the tips of the keys jutting between his fingers.

Fields does get out of the car but makes no move toward them; the engine's still running. He stands by his door to talk to Barker over the roof instead of through the window. Bewildered, he stares for a moment before forcing a smile. Then the smile becomes genuine.

"You kids are lucky," he says. "I'm in a good mood tonight. I'm not gonna book you after all." He shakes a finger at them. "Don't be doin' it in your car."

Fields drops back into the seat and the DeSoto's tires screech in the gutter. Barker sighs relief, realizing he's been holding his breath. In that moment before he steps into the street to try to catch the license plate, Fields disappears into the darkness.

Barker turns around to Margie. She's doing surprisingly well, considering.

"What just happened?" she says.

"I'm not sure," he says, though he's sure enough—and so is she. What just happened is something that happens to other people.

"We better find the police," she says.

They don't know where they're going but they walk anyway, without touching or speaking, both lost in thought until Barker flags down a passing car and asks where the nearest police station is. It's only a couple of blocks away—headquarters, the driver says, offering to take them. Barker declines the ride, and neither he nor Margie knows what to make of the fact that the man in the DeSoto pretending to be a cop had dropped them off within spitting distance of a real police station. Why had he taken that chance?

Before going inside, Margie pauses on the steps. "That was the most unusual blind date I've ever been on," she says. "Thank you for what you did."

Not until she later hears about some of Fields's less fortunate victims will Margie appreciate what the marine saved her from.

CHAPTER ELEVEN

Danny Galindo feels good. This is the best part of his job, telling victims that he's caught the bad guys, so they can start going on with their lives.

He was right, what he told that nice Baptist lady Annette V. Evans. It wasn't hard finding the creeps who gang-raped her. As he suspected, one of them tried pawning the camera, and all of them had bragged to someone who'd told someone who'd passed it on to someone who was trying to get out of a jam with a cop and figured it was a good trade. Danny showed the pawnbroker the three sketches. The pawnbroker picked out one, said he was sure, and within an hour Danny knew all three names. None had ever raped anyone, or at least none had ever been charged with rape, but each had been arrested multiple times, beginning in their teen years, for petty crimes and had spent time as guests of the city. Based on their rap sheets, Danny figured they were just buddies who'd heard this Baptist convention was being held at their old school, and with nothing else going on they dropped by to see what was happening. When opportunity knocked, they answered.

Danny and two street cops showed up at the first guy's parents' house with a warrant, found the purse in his closet, and by the time they cuffed him and said to say good-bye to Ma and Pa because he'd be going away till they were dead and buried, he was sobbing about how the whole thing was Ronald's idea and he just went along and didn't mean any harm. The usual. Well, he and his buds will have some time to think about it, but not as long as they would have if they'd insisted on taking this thing to trial instead of copping a plea—or if the victim had been white. If Miss Annette V. Evans had been white, these three idiots would be on death row in Quentin, and Danny's pretty sure he'd be getting a lot more slaps on the back for closing this thing out so fast.

The chatter around division isn't about him; it's about a street cop. A week ago Leonard Voss arrested two Negroes, Louie Rogers of Chicago and Cleo Steepers of nowhere in particular, for throwing four pot sticks from their car window when he was chasing them for speeding. The judge cut them loose on the grounds that the marijuana Voss stopped to pick up could've been anyone's; there was no way to verify whether the defendants had thrown something else out the window. Voss protested, the judge ordered him to shut up or be held in contempt, and Voss took a breather on the courthouse steps until Rogers and Steepers came out, when he promptly rearrested them on the same charge and drove them back to the station for rebooking. Now, after a little street justice administered below the neck, they're about to be arraigned again, again in front of Judge Joe Call, but this time Voss has threatened to quit the force and make a stink if charges are dismissed again. The law's not on Voss's side, but Chief Parker might be. Some guys are predicting that by the time Voss wakes up tomorrow, he might find himself promoted. At the least, he'll be called in to meet Parker for a wink and a nod and a smile and a two-handed shake. Maybe a snort. Voss is just the kind of cop Parker wants on his force breaking the rules in just the right way.

Or so it seems to the rank and file, but Danny wonders if the truth isn't a little more complicated and less dishonest. Most of the guys think Parker is someone he really isn't. They miss the point. But then again, it may be a point Parker *wants* them to miss. Truth is, he's no Klansman. He doesn't loathe Negroes on sight or feel superior to them personally or believe they're less entitled to scraps from the table than Bubba's good hunting dog. What keeps him up nights is the new Negro culture—sex, drugs, and rhythm and blues. Before the war, the area around Central Avenue was the kind of place you drove visitors from other countries to prove how well our dark-skinned citizens lived. They shopped, went to church, educated their children, worked for white people, knew their place and kept to it. Today, he seems to consider Darkville a malignancy.

It's not only getting bigger in L.A.—half again as big as before the war—it's spreading into the white world across the country; into white kids, who tomorrow will be white adults. Can it be a coincidence that that Elvis Presley is making millions singing the Negro's music while that Martin Luther King is down there in Montgomery, leading a bus boycott that's bringing a city to its knees and white people to his side? No, no coincidence. Parker reads the papers, listens to radio, watches television. He, too, followed the Nat King Cole attack a few months ago in Alabama, and unlike everyone else what he focused on was that in the original plot there were supposed to have been a hundred assailants—but only three dared to show up. And that the several hundred whites in that audience—Southerners!—gave the black man who was sharing the stage with a white band standing ovations both before and after the attack. Something's going on in this country. Hell, whites are trying to emulate Negroes in almost everything, from how they talk to what they wear. It's the Africanization of America, and it has to be slowed, even if it can't be stopped. Because when you take a whole quart of ice cream and stir in a little teaspoon of dogshit, the mix is going to taste a lot more like shit than ice cream.

Is that what Parker thinks? Danny doesn't know for sure but he believes it might be possible, because a lot of the cops are saying stuff like that and most of them aren't nifty enough to put all those factors together and spot a trend. So the word must be coming from on high, and in this department the conventional wisdom is whatever Chief William Parker says it is.

Besides, look at the way Parker treats his own Negroes. The LAPD is understaffed by two hundred officially and maybe five hundred in terms of public safety. It's ridiculous, a city this big with only four thousand sworn officers, less than a quarter of them on the street at any given time. Most places in L.A. you can drive for miles without ever seeing a black-and-white car on the street or a uniformed cop on the sidewalk. No wonder crime's going up so fast. If they wanted to, the bad guys could own every corner. So billboards all over town sell the LAPD as a great career choice, and the chief, whenever he speaks publicly—which he does all the time to civic groups—talks about how recruiting is one of his top priorities. He claims he's looking for the best men wherever he can find them. But he's not looking where he can find black men, that's for sure. And where he could find them if he bothered looking, joining the LAPD isn't much different from collaborating with Nazis. There aren't more than a few hundred blacks total in the department. They ride with each other or alone, never with whites, and work only in the traffic division or on the street in black areas (out of the Newton and Seventy-seventh Divisions) where, if they screw up, they're only screwing up their own—and taking the heat for being fascists. It may not actually be true, but it sometimes seems that Parker hopes the good Negro officers quit before he has to fire or promote them, the way he should've quit when he himself wasn't appreciated back in the bad old days. Right now the highest-ranking black is Rocky Washington, a lieutenant who's been a lieutenant since before Parker was a lieutenant—and was the first Negro lieutenant in the department's history; he'll probably die a lieutenant. Then there's Tom Bradley, who's only a sergeant, even though, like

Parker, he sucked it up through years of night law school and just got his degree. Chances are he'll quit out of frustration long before he commands anything more martial than the African Methodist Choir. Maybe he'll go practice law and defend Negroes against brutal cops. More likely he'll run for office. The way he turns the other cheek, this guy's got big-time ambitions that Parker can't see his way to capitalize on.

Danny hears cheers in the division. Loud, happy voices. Applause and whistles and whoops. Parker announced he was standing behind his guy Voss, and somehow when the two defendants were hauled back in front of Judge Call, the good judge saw fit to set bail conditions and a trial date for the Negroes who'd tossed the boo sticks.

Danny smiles at Miss Annette V. Evans. She thanks him for what he did, solving the case so quickly. Thank God, she won't have to come back for a trial. She says she can now work on forgiving them for what they did to her. But they haven't asked for forgiveness, Danny points out. They're only sorry for getting caught and going to prison.

Doesn't matter, she says. Danny's pretty sure that isn't exactly what Jesus had in mind when he said to forgive your enemies, but he's not the one who has to deal with getting raped.

"You don't want me to drive you to the airport?" he asks. "I'll get a squad car and we can run the siren." He knows she'll say no thanks, the Baptists insist, and he's glad when she does.

After she leaves, he pokes through some reports in the basket and sees a strange one, about a "huge Negro" posing as a cop who drove this young couple around, maybe intending to get rid of the male and rape the female. Maybe? Or probably? Danny wonders whether the answer has something to do with how you already think of Negro men. He knows what he thinks Parker thinks. He knows for sure what that desk sergeant thinks, because he knows her. But what does Danny himself think?

CHAPTER TWELVE

JURY DEBATES TWO DAYS ON DRUNK CHARGE

Wilson White, blind veteran, was found guilty late Wednesday on two counts of being drunk and of disturbing the peace.

The jury could not agree on the charges against his wife Mrs. Sally White and a retrial of those charges was set for Sept. 5.

The four men and eight women who made up the all-white jury deliberated for three days before returning White's guilty verdict. His lawyer vowed to appeal.

—An article that appeared in the *California Eagle* but not in any white newspaper— not the *Los Angeles Times*, the *Herald-Express*, the *Examiner*, the *Mirror*—during the summer of 1956.

CHAPTER THIRTEEN

Fields is sitting alone this Sunday night inside Ivie's Chicken and Meat on Firestone, scarfing down the combo plate with a cold Colt 45. He's a little self-conscious about eating by himself, the only one there not talking to someone, and the other conversations are too loud to pretend he's enjoying the radio being piped in. Too bad he can't hear it, Hunter Hancock's—Ol' H.H.—gospel show, *Songs of Soul and Spirit.* Fields loves gospel. Reminds him of being in church with his mom, rest her soul, the two of them singing in the choir. He'd been listening in the car on the way over, an album by some fourteen-year-old from Memphis named Aretha Franklin. "Precious Lord, Part 2" was on when he got out of the car. Now he thinks he can hear "While the Blood Runs Warm." The girl can sing.

From the next stool, Fields picks up a well-read copy of Thursday's *Sentinel.* On the front page is a shot of a man seemingly frozen midair in front of who knows what floor of a skyscraper. The caption reads, "Unusual photo shows Douglas Meservey, 51, jumping to his death from the 24th floor of the Russ Building in San Francisco last night, just as police entered building in effort to stop him. He leapt feet first to third floor roof. The Russ is the tallest building in the city."

Fields stares at the photo for a long time, wondering what it takes to jump off a building and why you'd do it and what you're thinking on the way down knowing you'll be dead in a second, before reading the story of the son of Eddie "Rochester" Anderson, Jack Benny's Negro, who's going to prison after getting caught with a few joints of tea. He thinks, *Man, if Jack Benny couldn't keep the kid out of Dutch, ain't no hope for no reg'lar folks.*

There's another article about an article in *Look* magazine by a white man who says that Negroes are better off in the South, where the racists are out in the open, than in the North, where Negroes only appear to be equal but in reality are confined to ghettos. There's an editorial about how California is one of nine states where Negroes can tip the balance of power in this upcoming election between Eisenhower and Stevenson, with Negroes likely to break for Eisenhower but friendly to Stevenson's message to Negroes.

Fields ignores them both for *Dot's Dashes,* the society column. His lips move as he reads who was at the "Stairway to the Stars" debutante ball and what they were wearing. He's never heard of any of them.

Then he gets to the classifieds—$10,000 new houses for sale, a grand down; tutoring for all ages, even adults, in English and math; night porter wanted in a downtown department store, and a certified magnaflux inspector at Cooper Products; a room at the Carver Hotel, nine bucks a week, including mirrored medicine cabinet, hot plate, retractable clothesline, and new Schlage locks. At the bottom of the page is an ad for a "very clean," used '49 Cadillac Fleetwood with thirty-four thousand miles—"forced to sell."

Forced to sell. Hmm. A Cadillac. Fleetwood. Wouldn't he look fine in one of those when he makes his rounds after midnight, cleaning the streets of morals violators, showing 'em how to love old Willie Roscoe?

What would that white fella say if he arrested him in a Caddie 'stead of a DeSoto?

He pays the check and walks out to the phone booth on the sidewalk, the page turned to the Caddy ad—which is on the same page as a display ad with a drawing of a young couple, at home, using a telephone. He stops to read it.

"Here's a picture of a family about to start a pleasant weekend vacation," says the ad copy. "And here's how they planned it. His wife called the sports shop to see that their tennis rackets were restrung. She phoned the cleaners', too, about that suit she wanted to wear. And they arranged by telephone for the neighbors to feed the cat. He called ahead for reservations and they're off. Sure, this is a special occasion. But even if it's every day, the telephone is always ready to do so many things, so quickly and with so much convenience. The men and women of Pacific Telephone work to make your telephone more useful every day."

Hmm, having his own telephone. Never thought about it before. It's a nice thought—as long as they don't give him an Axminster number, and they probably would in that part of town. Even if he could remember it, he wouldn't be able to tell it to anybody. For some reason, the word *Axminster* will not come out of his mouth in a way anybody would recognize. A few weeks ago at work the guys split a gut when he tried reading the number on the dispatcher's business card, his tongue getting more tied every time he tried, which made it funnier. Still, having a phone might be something. Maybe he'll call the number to inquire. Maybe they'd give him a Dunkirk number. He can say Dunkirk. How smooth would it be to have not only a Caddie but a phone, too?

He closes the booth door, drops a dime, dials AX 3-3938.

A man answers. Fields says he's calling about the Cadillac Fleetwood he saw advertised in the *Sentinel*. He uses his best standard English, even though this is another Negro who doesn't speak much better than he does. The man tells him about the miles, that it's clean and well maintained—nothing Fields doesn't already know from reading the ad. "Do you want to drive it?" the man asks.

"Yeah," Fields say. "But it says you forced to sell."

"Yeah."

"What's that mean? Who forcing you?"

"What're you talkin' 'bout?" the man asks. He's getting pissed.

"Someone makin' you sell? Who?"

"Money! I'm sellin' 'cause I need the money. Get it?"

"Oh, yeah," Fields says. "I get it. Two-door or four?"

"Four."

"That's good."

"And it's got a V-8."

"That's good, too. What color?"

"Cream."

"I like that." Pause. "Hundred bucks."

"Huh?"

"What?"

"Did you say a hundred bucks?"

"Yeah, I'll give you a hundred."

"Hundred bucks?"

"Cash."

"You fuckin' with me, Johnson? I paid three thousand six hundred and fifty-two dollars."

"You say you need money."

"Stupid ni—"

The man hangs up.

Unless he steals one, Willie Fields won't be driving a Cadillac Fleetwood anytime soon.

CHAPTER FOURTEEN

Danny rarely sees Chief Parker more than in passing down the hall or whatever, but he often sees him doing just that. They say hello, how's it going, usually nothing more. This time the chief asks Danny into his office for a few minutes, says there's something he wants his opinion on. What it could be, Danny has no idea.

Danny knows more about Chief William Parker than the chief knows about Danny. Which is something, because Parker supposedly keeps a dossier about everyone but hardly ever talks about himself—unless, that is, he's been drinking. Which means every night, pretty much, and almost every day there's a chance that "Whisky Bill, as he was affectionately known, might let a tidbit slip to whoever happens to be there. Anyway, when you're the chief of police of Los Angeles, and you scratched and clawed and climbed up your own ambition for two and a half decades before the Police Commission finally voted you chief, you can't help leaving some clues for men who are paid to look, watch, see, hear, deduce, conclude, and report. Word has a way of getting around among those who know better than anyone else that no one's perfect.

Then there's the fact that the guy Parker beat out six years ago for chief was Thad Brown. He's chief of detectives and still bitter that three of the five commission members were openly committed to him before Parker found ways to delay their vote until the breast cancer that he knew was killing the lady in Brown's camp finally took her. Sure, it was dirty, but wrangling that fifth vote from the dead lady's replacement before Brown could get to him proved that Parker was better equipped for the job. Results are what matter.

Danny respects Brown—and then some—but understands that the impossible job of professionalizing the LAPD and managing to alchemize it from corrupt cesspool to anything better requires more than brains. It takes an ability to make people believe that you're the only person who can get other people to believe what they don't believe and don't want to believe. Parker, not Brown, does that.

William H. Parker had come to Los Angeles from Deadwood, South Dakota, with his divorced mother—who'd finally left his real-S.O.B. father—and three younger brothers in 1922. He was seventeen, and in most ways L.A. looked more like the Wild West than even Deadwood. Parker loved it at first sight. He wasn't alone. Every day thousands were coming from all over the country, running from their pasts to where they thought the future was being built. And it was, by anyone with the gumption to stick it out. Parker soon married a woman he later accused in a jealous rage of having birthed a child by another man. When she pointed out that the kid she was cradling in her arms was her sister's, he was contrite enough not to beat her. But he had before, and she was smart to leave. Like his father, Parker was a mean drunk.

From the beginning, he wallowed in ambition. He intended to be a lawyer, which from the looks of things was a profession that led anywhere he might want to go, supporting his new wife and paying for night-school law classes by driving a taxi. That turned out to be the perfect fit. During Prohibition, the front seat of a cab was just the vantage from which to see who was doing what, where, and how to whom, and the view squashed every dying vestige of the notion that man had been born anything other than wicked. If L.A. was a machine, the grease on its gears was corruption. And cops threw the starter switch.

For whatever reason, maybe because he had some Irish in him, and maybe because his grandfather had been a top cop in Deadwood before getting elected to Congress and dying of cirrhosis, cops fascinated Parker. Most of them were uneducated galoots and thugs, which meant police work was a first resort and line of least resistance. These were not the men you deployed to the ramparts when the bad guys mounted an attack, nor the ones to be that thin blue line, as he put it, between civilization and anarchy. At any given moment you could hear the screams of men in holding cells being beaten into confessing to crimes that others had paid not to pay for. Danny has always wondered what made Parker begin thinking he had a future in police work longer than next week.

The bigger mystery was what then made Parker different from everyone who'd come before him, most of whom had no doubt been raised to do good by doing right in God-fearing families. Why had Parker decided not to reap the rewards of jumping in the craphole along with the other cops at a time when the only way to the top was through the bottom? Why had he chosen to remain incorruptible? You only had to have met Parker once to know that, with his brains and smarts, he could've risen quickly through the ranks, made chief, filled mattresses with retirement dough, driven cars and lived in homes paid for by others, then someday been elected mayor. Maybe better than that. All he had to do was play by the rules already in place.

But from Parker's first days in the department, in 1927, he made enemies.

And they were the worst kind of enemies. They were enemies with power who became enemies because they think you think you're morally superior. It's not anything you say; it's what you don't do. And what you don't do is wink and nod and hold out your hand for your share. To them, being incorruptible is a sick kind of corruption. It doesn't make you trustworthy. It makes you suspect.

One of his first arrests was of a news reporter with a bottle of booze in his car, this being Prohibition. The guy laughed as Parker dragged him into the Central Division station. The sergeant on duty told Parker to let the man go. Parker refused, the sergeant shrugged, the reporter found himself in court, Parker sat waiting to testify, and the judge dismissed the case after a police captain testified to giving the reporter the booze—some good hooch it was, too, he said.

Parker was at the right place at the right time when he spotted a guy on a street with a woman's fur coat under his arm. Parker asked where he was going. The guy told him to piss off. Now Parker remembered reading the description of a male suspect wanted in San Francisco for cutting up some people. Patting the man down, Parker found a long-bladed knife and brought him in. Parker's captain didn't take the news well. Protocol said that this should've been his collar; the rookie should've had the sense to hand the cutter over and let an officer of high rank pad his file. So the following week, when some shop owner was holding two of his own employees hostage with a shotgun, the captain made sure Parker was the cop to take the call. And for the second time, the captain was disappointed to see Parker return safely to the station instead of getting his head blown off—which was what the shooter would've done had Parker not outwitted him. That Parker had walked in alive was bad enough. But to bring another collar with him was too much to bear.

Parker kept acing the civil service tests. They couldn't help but promote him. He made enemies as much inside the divisions as on the street, where he refused to go along with the protection rackets. One time he parked himself in uniform in front of a whorehouse run by a lady who asked why she, out of the other jillion brothels in the city paying to have the cops pretend they were invisible, was being singled out to have her johns scared.

"You stupid ass," she told him, "you're ruining my business."

"That's the idea," Parker said.

That got him another transfer, and another followed that.

Parker didn't have friends in high places, but firing him was impossible with his off-the-chart test scores. By the time World War II started, Parker had earned his law degree and saw a way to do bigger things than be sergeant in charge of traffic division, even if ten times more Angelenos were dying in their cars than from murder.

He made inquiries in Washington and was promised a captain's commission and rapid advance, possibly a colonel's command by the end of the war. His wife was thrilled for him, and maybe herself, too, as Parker jumped on a train.

When he got back East, however, he discovered that he'd been commissioned a first lieutenant, not a captain, and had to console himself with the pleasure of spending some months studying at Harvard before being shipped off to North Africa.

Just after D-day, he was wounded slightly above the right eye by a German fighter plane. The Purple Heart was no substitute for his slow advancement, so when he read that crime in L.A. had doubled, tripled, quadrupled since the war began, he tried resigning his commission and getting sent home. His talents, he thought, would finally be welcomed.

Which simply proved just how much he'd forgotten during his absence about life and politics in the City of Angels. Whoever heard of someone going off to war and getting *less* cynical? It turned out that LAPD chief Horrall, who still had some pull at the Pentagon, was more concerned with protecting his seat on the throne than with his city's crime rate. The army refused to demobilize Parker. He was going to have to tough it out till the end, but even then the army still wouldn't let him go. He spent two years remaking the police departments in German cities, where nothing was as it seemed, and no one could be trusted.

It was the kind of experience you couldn't buy anywhere. At any cost. Now, he believed, the LAPD would have to deal with him on his own terms, no matter how corrupt or self-interested the brass were. The tide of history was at last moving his way. Here he was on the precipice of a new era, a decorated war hero, a man trusted with emergency powers in a devastated country who'd left behind functioning police departments, the last man home and the highest-ranking LAPD officer to serve in the war. That put him in position to see better than anyone else what the hordes of veterans streaming into Los Angeles every month were doing to the city. And he knew what to do about it.

William H. Parker began working the press, the American Legion, the city council, the mayor, and especially the public. He gave more speeches and shook more hands than any political candidate and did it all with a messiah's effectiveness. You just had to admire the man's devotional ambition. In the end, he won. And owed his job as chief to the votes of one Negro commissioner and one Jew commissioner. True, their choices were limited to two white men, but Parker kept his word and promoted to sergeant, strictly on merit, a Negro policewoman whose test scores were high and service commendable—the first colored lady to climb that high in the department's hundred years.

"Detective Galindo," Parker says. "Thank you for coming in."

"Chief."

"I want to ask you something and get your opinion."

"All right, Chief."

"And we'll keep it between us, if you don't mind."

"Yes, sir."

"Danny," Parker says, "I'm thinking about desegregating the department."

Danny's eyes widen because he doesn't know how to widen his ears or replay what he just heard. On a list of a million things he could've imagined Parker talking to him about, this has to be nine hundred thousand something. He can't help thinking back a week or so ago to the joke he overheard a uniform tell some other cops in a voice that wasn't trying to keep it down: "So these two niggers run into each other in the street, and one says, 'Hey, man, what's yo name?' And the other one says, 'George Washington Carver.' 'George Washington Carver? That's my name, too.' 'Yeah? How you spell it?' 'X, X, X—George Washington Carver.' 'X, X, X? Dat's how I spell my name, too. X, X, X, X, X.' 'Huh?' says the first one. 'X, X, X, X, X? What dose two otha X's fo?' 'George Washington Carver, Attorney at Law.' " All the cops laughed hard and long, no courtesy laughs in the bunch, and since then—once in a cop bar, once in a chop suey restaurant in Chinatown—Danny's seen two more cops try to tell it, but both times they were stopped when the other person said he'd already heard it.

Danny works to keep the shock out of his voice. "You're thinking about desegregating?"

"Yes, integrating," Parker says.

Danny is confused. He knows that Parker's official stance is that the department is already integrated, even though colored and white don't ride together and coloreds are assigned to their own neighborhoods. He knows that Parker sent his own undercover guys to observe city council meetings where integration of the fire and police departments were discussed. And he remembers Parker's reaction last year when the fire chief, Alderson, was fired for telling them to piss off after they ordered him to let white firemen and black firemen share the same flames; no way, he said, was he going to send white firemen to black areas and black firemen to white areas. What Parker did was insist that the council had no business meddling in his business, that if they wanted their city to be as safe as it could be, they'd shut up and let him do what he'd been hired to do. And, according to the city charter, couldn't be fired for doing.

It suddenly occurs to Danny what might be on Parker's mind. The other day a federal court in Alabama—of all places—ruled that the Jim Crow laws keeping Negroes from riding in the front of the bus weren't constitutional. So all those people boycotting the buses in Montgomery over this were winning. Maybe the city would appeal to the Supreme Court, and maybe it wouldn't. If it did, judging by what these same justices said about segregated education a couple of years before, the ruling would stand. And Parker would know that. He'd know, probably better than anybody, that this is all a sand castle. Each time the tide comes in, a little more of it's washed away, till finally you can't see it was ever there.

"You mean, black and white together?" Danny says.

"Yes."

"Same car?"

"Yes."

"Same beat?"

"Yes."

Danny takes a deep breath, not because he's thinking but because he wants Parker to think he's thinking—though he's pretty sure Parker's smarter than he is and knows that Danny's only pretending to think this through instead of just coming out and saying what he's believed for a long time.

"Chief," Danny says, "it's inevitable."

Parker lets Danny hang for a moment. "Thank you for your candor, Detective," he says. "I appreciate your coming in."

Danny goes back to work, wondering if Parker has been hitting the bottle early.

CHAPTER FIFTEEN

MAN PARALYZED AFTER GRAPPLING WITH POLICEMAN

A 38-year-old presser is in General Hospital, his right side paralyzed as a result of what he claimed was a beating given him by an off-duty policeman.

Willie C. Washington, of 1537½ 6th Ave., stated that the officer, identified as William McMonagle, hit him from the back Thursday night, and that after he had fallen, the officer held him pinned to the ground by putting his foot on his face.

Officer McMonagle insisted that Washington was trying to resist arrest but did not disclose what the arrest was for.

"I was just minding my own business," Washington said from his hospital bed. "Why'd he have to do me like that? I wouldn't of done him that way (like that)."

—From an article that appeared in the *California Eagle* but not in any white newspaper—not the *Los Angeles Times,* the *Herald-Express,* the *Examiner,* the *Mirror*—during the summer of 1956.

CHAPTER SIXTEEN

It's twenty after one in the morning. Miko Kihara and Steve Tanaka lost track of the time after stopping near Lafayette Park in his father's late-model Chevy. She's nineteen, a UCLA student studying history. He's twenty-one, fresh out of USC, an accountant in the receivables department of Bullock's Wilshire, where even with the employee discount he can't yet afford the clothes let alone the furniture. They can both remember their childhood internments at Manzanar, though without much bitterness except for the two years when their fathers enlisted in the war effort and were sent to Europe. No matter. They lost their homes anyway and had had to start over. That was how it was, and sometimes how it was wasn't fair. Even in America. There was no point complaining. But if their still-traditional families discovered them fondling each other in a lovers' lane, like white American teens who live with their parents and have no other place for romance, they would feel deeply shamed. And if the police discovered them, the stain of dishonor could never be washed out in this lifetime.

No matter that they're in love and engaged to wed.

Miko stiffens at the sight of the tall black man outside the car holding a flashlight in one hand and a badge in the other. The flashlight beam covers her face. Steve sees the terror in her eyes and whips his head around, pivots on his seat, opens the door, and stands at attention alongside the car.

"Sir?" Steve says. Fields is almost a foot taller.

"What're you doing in there?" Fields asks. "Making love?"

"Oh, no, no, no. No, sir," Steve says in what's left of a voice robbed by panic. It's Fields's authority, not his towering size, that frightens him.

"Well, I says you were, and that's violating the law," Fields says. "Looks like it's a big night. I just got through with another nice young couple who don't care to uphold the law." He leans down and looks past Steve into the Chevy. "Out of the car, young lady."

Trembling, Miko slides across the front seat and stands next to her boyfriend. Until now, Fields thought all Japs looked alike. But this one's special, and at just over five feet tall—well, for a moment he's lost in the possibilities.

"You are certainly a pretty young thing," he says. "I can see where your young man here might want to take advantage of you."

"He wasn't taking advantage of me," she insists. There's no apology or fear in her voice. But she feels it and doesn't know how to stop it from controlling her face.

Fields turns to Steve, his smile now a scowl. "You're goin' to jail, boy. You see that car there?" Fields points to the DeSoto, partially hidden behind a palm-tree trunk twenty yards away. "It's an undercover car—*my* undercover car. That's what you're going to jail in. And don't be thinkin' 'bout running away."

Steve sadly shakes his head and looks over at Miko, pursing his lips in an invisible promise that it's going to be okay. Her chin stops quivering until he turns his back when Fields grabs his shoulder to guide him toward the car.

"I'm gonna radio for another car to pick you up," he tells her. "Stay right here."

He marches Steve, thinking that this time he's got the perfect plan.

Fields puts Steve in the shotgun seat. Steve watches him shut the door. The way he holds his hands on his lap, they may as well have been handcuffed.

Fields gets in and they pull away. As they pass, Steve sees Miko standing alone and wonders if he'll ever see her again.

"Ever been in jail?" Fields asks.

"Not exactly," Steve says.

"What's that mean?"

"I spent three years in an internment camp?"

"In Europe?" Fields asks.

"No, here in California."

Fields looks puzzled. No matter. He's not listening anymore anyway. He pulls to the curb at Sixth and Grand View. It's a quiet residential street, and dark. They've gone only half a mile. He says, "I can see you're truly sorry for what you done, so I'm giving you a break. Get out."

"Excuse me?"

"Get out."

Steve opens the door but doesn't move. "Here? But what about Miko?"

"You want me to drag you out?"

Steve says, "I, I don't understand." But now he does understand, when Fields's big hand pushes him onto the sidewalk.

Fields presses the accelerator to the floor, the car's velocity slamming the door shut. Steve trails the exhaust before realizing that he's running the wrong way. He turns and sprints back toward his car.

Fields has gone around the block. Miko wears her purse on her shoulder. She sees the DeSoto coming, and Steve's not in it. It's been less than five minutes.

To Fields, pulling beside the Chevy, Miko looks like she's waiting for a bus.

"You still here?" he asks. "Good, get in."

She opens the door for herself and climbs in, part of her realizing that something's not right and wondering why she's going along with this. "Where's Steve?" she wants to know.

Fields shakes his head in a scold, checks his rearview mirror, and they drive off.

"Where's Steve?" she asks again.

Fields doesn't feel like saying anything, but the way he's saying nothing tells Miko more than she wants to hear—and everything she already knew. Every moment that passes, every car and building and streetlamp they pass, means that she's that much closer to something she can't even imagine and therefore can't prepare herself for. It will be a horror, that much she knows.

"I'm very sorry," she says.

"Yeah."

"What will become of us?" Miko asks.

"That for the judge to decide," Fields says.

She knows that's not how he means it, but as a believing Presbyterian, she can't help but remember that the Judge really will decide whether she goes to heaven or hell, and He may be making that decision soon, because right now she's not sure she'll be allowed to live after what's about to happen. Still, it's almost funny, this man still thinking that she doesn't know he's not a cop—and her ever thinking he was.

"Yes," she says softly.

Just past Western Avenue, Fields pulls into a darkened alley strewn with garbage. He parks, turns off the engine, pushes in the headlights knob.

Miko had closed her eyes, so she didn't see Fields actually putting the knife to her neck; now she knows what a switchblade opening sounds like. She stares sideways at him. Something that feels like a scream wants to come out of her throat but doesn't. It can't.

"Take off your clothes," he says, now just letting her see the knife.

She has no will to resist and tries to unbutton her blouse. Her hands are trembling too much.

"Here," he says. He puts the knife in his lap and, starting from the top, undoes each button with the tenderness of a groom on his virgin bride's wedding night. Her brain is so foggy she doesn't even consider reaching quickly for the open knife and stabbing him somewhere.

Now Fields places one hand behind her and easily unlatches her brassiere. He drags the blouse off her arms and leaves it crumpled behind her before sliding the bra straps off her shoulders, staring at the reveal of her breasts. Jap tits. Yes. He cups them in his hands and grunts with approval and anticipation.

Miko watches all this from somewhere outside herself.

"Your pants," he says.

They're pedal pushers, tight and difficult to get off. He uses one hand to undo the top button, then she moves his hand away to unzip them herself. She shimmies them down, leaning back into the seat to lift her hips. Only her underwear remains, and now not that.

Miko wishes she hadn't noticed that Fields's zipper is open, and he's stroking himself, fully erect. She can't imagine she'll survive that thing in her.

"Climb over, get in the backseat," he says.

She does as she's told, and for the few moments that she's back there alone while he removes his pants, she clamps her knees shut and crosses her arms across her chest. It does no good.

The ordeal ends with a thundering groan.

Fields lifts her off him and rests with his head against the upholstery, breathing hard, then grinning. Proud of himself.

In the corner, Miko curls herself into a fetal ball, her body convulsing. She wishes he really had cut her throat and almost hopes he will now.

Fields watches her for a moment. "Didn't you like it?" he asks.

When she doesn't answer, he snaps at her to get dressed. And when she doesn't move, he leans forward and reaches into the front seat for her clothes, dropping them on her.

"Unless you wanna go another round," he snaps, pissed that she's not cooing.

Miko dresses deliberately, making sure everything's in place, still watching herself from afar, wondering how this is all going to end.

She hasn't even realized that they're driving now.

"You hungry?" Fields asks. "I am."

He pulls up to the curb by Ivie's Chicken and Meat near Forty-fifth and Hoover and jumps out. Miko sits shivering—and then is startled by his face at her open window.

"Well, look, girl," he says, "if you ain't gonna eat with me, then don't be here when I get back. Here"—he pulls out a buck from his pocket and throws it at her—"get a cab to wherever you goin'."

She's already gone when he returns with two chili dogs, a trough of fries, and a Coca-Cola. He turns on the radio and begins eating. Now KGFJ is on the air, Johnny Magnus introducing "Night Owl" by Tony Allen. "So long, night owl, so long. Yes, baby, well, well, well. Be on your merry way." Magnus comes back and says he's got a special treat for all his night owls, a demo hot off the presses of a new Little Richard song.

"Hey," Fields says, putting a fry in his mouth. "I saw him myself. Little Richard."

"Drink it in, night owls," Magnus says, "'cause you may not hear it again for a while if the censors get their hands on it. This little beauty is called 'Jenny Jenny.'"

"'Jenny, Jenny,'" Fields repeats. "Mmm, mmm." From the first bars, Fields likes it. He likes it a lot.

"Spinnin' spinnin' spinnin', spinnin' like a spinnin' top. Spinnin' spinnin', ooh, spinnin' spinnin'."

"Let's let the good times roll," Magnus says, playing the song back-to-back-to-back for all his night owls.

"Let 'em roll, baby," Fields says before singing along.

CHAPTER SEVENTEEN

The young Japanese woman tells her story of being abducted and raped by a Negro man who said he was a policeman. She stares down at the counter, eyes unfocused, simply describing what happened to her as if it had happened to someone else—just the way she survived the ordeal.

A young Japanese man, who also says he has a story to relate about what the Negro man did, stands at a respectful distance, pretending that his girlfriend is behind a kind of shoji screen for privacy.

Lorraine Olson, the desk sergeant, listens and takes notes, nodding her head and asking a few questions that weren't otherwise answered. She's exasperated that these Nips waited three goddamned days to come forward, and that Miko washed her clothes, meaning there's no chance of finding hairs or fibers or anything else that might help. They didn't get the guy's license plate, either.

She says, "You weren't the first."

For the first and only time, Miko looks directly at her.

Olson calls Detective Carpenter over and introduces him to Miko and Steve. Carpenter has worked a hundred rape cases, maybe a thousand, but this MO rings a loud bell. He's as horrified as he is excited by the thought that someone out there has been inspired by Caryl Chessman. On any given day, there's a newspaper or TV story about Chessman in his cell on death row in San Quentin, sentenced to death eight years ago for putting a phony cop light atop a stolen car and shining it at cars parked on lovers' lanes, then robbing young women, and, in the case of one seventeen-year-old, forcing her to blow him. He was supposed to have been gassed years ago for kidnapping—that is, dragging her that short distance from her car—and causing "great bodily harm" by leaving that taste in her mouth forever. But Chessman turned into an amazing jailhouse lawyer and the author of three bestselling books, so he's had more stays of execution than Carpenter can remember. The whole world, according to the newspapers, is on that little arrogant piece of shit's side. Foreign diplomats and leaders, American politicians, famous actors and writers—they all want his death sentence not only commuted but the cell door opened forever. And you know what? That just may happen. And now some Negro who knows how to read may have picked up *Cell 2455, Death Row*. No, never mind, he probably saw the movie that came out last year and thought, *Yeah, that's how it's done*. This is a big deal.

"I told you that that's what the guy intended with that other couple," Olson tells Carpenter. "That other girl got off lucky." Now she realizes what she's said in front of Miko and adds, "Sorry."

Carpenter leads the couple to an interview room, sits them side by side in gunmetal chairs by a gunmetal desk, and has them wait while he goes somewhere. Miko and Steve don't speak and don't glance at each other.

Carpenter comes back in with Danny Galindo. They lay some books filled with mug shots on the table and explain what they need from her. Miko pauses, no one sure what she'll do. She reaches for the first and opens its cover.

Danny notices how she's taking her time with each page, not wanting to see the guy who did this to her and yet not not wanting to either. That's interesting. No photo has made her hesitate for even half a heartbeat. It might mean the guy's face is branded on her brain and all Negroes don't look alike to her. Or it could mean nothing.

There are a lot more whites in Los Angeles than blacks, and there are more blacks than whites in these books. What does that mean?

Miko gets through the first few and can't say that any of them resemble the man who did this to her. Steve mostly takes his lead from her, agreeing that nothing has struck him either.

Danny tells them to flip through the books again, if they're up to it. The boyfriend and girlfriend really shouldn't be doing this together, but Danny isn't sure he'd get a good read from either of them alone. He's been watching both faces to see if one reacts and the other doesn't; that'll tell him something. So far, nothing.

In a while Miko points to one and says, "I don't know, maybe," then does the same two pages before the last page of the last book.

She flips back one at a time to the two she narrowed down, her head moving right to left to right to left half a dozen times before she stops and says, "I can't be sure, but I don't think so."

"I don't either," Steve agrees.

"Let's go over the story again," Carpenter says. "Moment by moment, one moment at a time."

"But this time *you* tell it," Danny says to Steve, then turns to Miko. "Please, no help."

Steve begins with when he picked up Miko in his father's Chevy. Carpenter explains he should start at the point just before the bad guy got there. Steve is having trouble couching what he and Miko were doing with each other when Danny interrupts, asking, "Did he touch your car— the roof or door?"

"Maybe, I don't know," Steve says. "Yes, I think."

"Is your car here?" Danny asks.

"It's with my dad. At work."

"We're going to have to dust the car for fingerprints, so . . ."

Steve looks nervously at Miko. Her eyes widen in fear.

"Ah, I don't think he touched the car," Steve says. "Yes, I remember now, he didn't touch the car. He hit on the window with his flashlight. That's what got our attention. And I think that my father already washed his car since the other night. He takes good care of it."

Danny sighs. There's a huge Negro out there doing bad things, and chances are he's had run-ins with the law before in California. A fingerprint match could end this quickly.

Steve tells the rest of what he knows through to where he chased the DeSoto. That's as far as he can go. From there it's Miko's story, and you can see the failure and humiliation on Steve's face as she talks. When this is all said and done, it may be Steve who has the hardest time coping with how foolish and inept and weak he feels over not being able to protect his girlfriend, maybe someday his wife, when she needed him most.

Danny gives Carpenter the look. There isn't much more to go on than what they already had from that lady Margie and her date, the marine— other than confirmation that the guy would've raped her if the marine hadn't figured it out.

They've got artist's sketches of what Margie and the marine remembered. But Miko and Steve agreed that the bad guy doesn't have anything memorable to distinguish him, like a limp or a scar on his cheek or gap between his teeth; right now he could be any of ten thousand six-foot-four Negroes.

They know he drives an older DeSoto, dark with red upholstery. But L.A. has twenty thousand DeSotos, half fitting the description.

They have two lovers' lanes a mile and half apart in mostly white neighborhoods, and L.A. has dozens more, maybe hundreds.

Danny asks the sketch artist to come in and, as with Margie and the marine, to work the sketches separately.

Soon there are four sketches, all of them similar enough to pick any of them as the one to work from.

Danny escorts the couple as far as the front desk and looks at Miko when he says he'll be in touch with any news or questions.

Miko glances at Steve, who quickly asks whether they'd please please call him whenever they do call, for either of them, at his work number. "Wait, on second thought"—he realizes it's not much better to have the police call there than home, then realizes that not much better is still better—"no, that's right."

Danny says he understands, he'll do just that, and then he walks over to Carpenter's desk. He doesn't hear Lorraine Olson ask Miko and Steve to hold on a second while she reaches into a drawer.

"What do you think?" Carpenter says.

Danny shakes his head. "A real son of a bitch," he says.

"The case or the guy?"

"He's gotta have a name, he's gotta live somewhere," Danny says. He stares at one of the sketches. "Someone has to know him."

"Why isn't he raping Negro girls?" Carpenter says.

"Maybe he is," Danny says. "But until something comes in, we can figure that he's doing it in better neighborhoods because he doesn't want to be recognized in his own. Someone knows him. Someone'll recognize him."

"What, you're going door-to-door—fifty thousand houses? Not me."

"We'll run the sketch in the newspapers."

"Forget it. They won't run it."

"Why do you say that?"

"The Negro papers. He's one of their own."

"Come on, they're always running crime," Danny says. "And this one's got it all—rapist terrorizing lovers' lanes."

"You're being naïve. This is a nigger sex maniac and the victims aren't."

Danny ignores the slur, knowing they probably have a few choice names for the Mexican when he's not around, too. He says, "So we'll give it to the *Times* or *Mirror* or *Herald-Express,* all of them. I'll take it down to the PIO"—public information office.

"For what?" Carpenter says. "How's that do any good?"

Danny pauses a second and says, "Just because whites don't read black papers doesn't mean blacks don't read ours."

"What do you mean *ours*?"

He's kidding. Danny knows that. Or does he? Maybe Carpenter thinks Danny changes into a zoot suit before curling up on the sofa with *La Opinión.*

"It's your case," Danny says. "Your lead. Whatever you say." He walks away. It's not his case.

CHAPTER EIGHTEEN

HOME BOMBED; TWO YOUNG GIRLS ESCAPE DEATH

PLACENTIA—Threat of trouble which has been brooding over this small community ever since Gerald Harris, San Pedro shipyards worker, bought a home at 133 Missouri St., exploded into open violence Monday night when night riders tossed a homemade bomb into a bedroom in which Harris's two young daughters were sleeping. Another bomb landed on the front lawn.

Neither of the two girls was injured when the exploding bomb—a bottle filled with gasoline—set fire to the furniture and ringed the girls' bed with a wall of flame.

"It's just a miracle that I have my two little girls today," the bewildered Harris said as he surveyed the damage and wondered aloud how "anybody could do a thing like this."

—An article that appeared in the *California Eagle* but not in any white newspaper— not the *Los Angeles Times,* the *Herald-Express,* the *Examiner,* the *Mirror*—during the summer of 1956.

CHAPTER NINETEEN

Todd Roark tidies up his tidy little home, two bedrooms and bath, that he rents on Thirty-seventh, just west of Normandie. It's a pleasant enough neighborhood for Negroes, most of the little houses built in the 1920s for a different class, the lawns still tended and green.

He always cleans the place a little extra when he gets his little girl, Teri Denise, and it's not often enough because he doesn't have custody and has to beg her mom for a night here and there, and usually she says no—if she even takes the call. The woman spits and sweats hate for him. He knows there's not a moment of the day, if she thinks about it, she doesn't want to see him dead—or better, suffering. So dealing with her isn't exactly pleasant.

Still, it's worth all the hell if he gets to see Teri Denise for even an hour. He adores his little girl, even if he doesn't adore her mom anymore. Things soured fast. He and Thelma Dailey, they'd had a wild courtship, all right, one that ended half an hour or so after they learned she was pregnant with Teri Denise—which was thirteen months before they divorced. If only reality hadn't intruded, they might've had one of the

great love affairs, something from a movie. Instead it became one of
those Saturday-afternoon horror matinees about an atomic creature. *Ir-
reconcilable differences* doesn't hint at the problems that real life
brought to their marriage, or whatever you want to call the time they had.
That gun to his head forcing him to say *I do,* Todd held it himself, then
fired the bullet, wanting to do what's right even though he knew he'd
probably end up doing what was wrong. And he did, sooner rather than
later, by not being faithful during Thelma's pregnancy. But he doesn't
like to think about that.

What he likes thinking about is his little angel, Teri. She'll be two in a
couple of months, and he could never have imagined loving anyone or
anything this way. Sure, his own mom, who lives a few miles away, loves
him that way. But that doesn't count, not the way he sees it. She's a churchgoing woman who thinks Jesus listens to her prayers and will make good
things happen as long as she's worthy of them. Which is just foolishness.
Because if ever a woman was worthy, Julia Roark is worthy, no bribes
necessary—and what does she have? Not nearly enough.

It's a little before five. Todd wipes the dust from the clock in his living room. He's supposed to pick up Teri Denise at Thelma's in a few
minutes, just before Thelma's new boyfriend picks her up. He takes a
last check of the place. It looks pretty good, about as good as it can look.
On the coffee table he straightens the pile of manuals and books he's
been studying to get his private investigator's license, hides the cloth
he's been using to dust in the stove, and picks up his coat.

A knock comes just as he opens the door, and sees three cops standing on the little porch. He recognizes two of them from the Seventy-
seventh, where he worked traffic for four years and, if he hadn't gotten
fired, might've spent another forty doing the same.

"Todd Roark?" asks Garland, who knows goddamned well it's Todd
Roark.

"Bill, what's going on?"

"You have to come with us."

"Why?"

Why? Because on their way out of the station, Miko and Steve were stopped by Lorraine Olson, who showed them the academy graduation close-up of Roark in his crisp police uniform and service cap and asked, "Is this the person who raped you?"

Well, maybe it was, Miko said, and then Steve said, maybe it was.

"Just please come with us," Garland tells Todd. He doesn't really mean please.

"I have to pick up my daughter," Todd says.

"Not now," Morgan says.

"Am I under arrest for something?" Todd asks. He can't imagine that he is, but you can't rule anything out. He feels a little sick and scared but knows they can't take him in without his consent unless they arrest him. On the other hand, what's strictly legal and what they'll do anyway is academic. There's no point debating. These are foot soldiers carrying out orders. Someone told them to do this. They can't be reasoned with.

And no, they won't let him make a quick call before leaving. So he goes, pretending in case his neighbors see that he's being picked up by some old buddies in their black-and-white. He asks if he can get in front. They at least let him have that. Morgan climbs in back. Garland drives. Todd tries to find out what's going on, but both guys are all business. One thing's for sure: whatever this is, it ain't good.

Todd Roark has spent much of his life ignoring the faces of people who he thinks look like they want to hurt him. Or worse. But this is different. Inside the station, every cop he passes looks like he'd stand in line to pull the trigger, even at his already riddled corpse. Olson, he can see, would love to horsewhip him, just like in the good old days when her ancestors were doing that to his.

Turns out he's being accused of rape and kidnapping on July 20 and 30.

"What? Are you kidding?"

The thought is ludicrous. Absurd. Ridiculous. And if he hadn't once been a member in good standing of the LAPD, Todd Roark might've laughed when Detective Carpenter told him. But he'd seen plenty of guys more innocent than the average cop sent away for a long time, pleading guilty to crimes they hadn't committed to avoid even worse punishment doled out by juries who believe cops don't make mistakes and would never lie—or if they would, for a good reason only. That's why he sneaks in a call to his attorney, the one who was so useless when he was getting fired, instead of Teri Denise. Teri's mom thinks he's an asshole anyway, so that's what she'll figure when he doesn't show up tonight.

He's in an interview room, pacing, nervous, when Carpenter walks in and closes the door behind him.

"I didn't do whatever you think I did," Todd says. "You know that."

"No, I don't," Carpenter says.

No, he doesn't know that. Todd can see it on his face. To Carpenter, a Negro man sleeping with white women is a Negro capable of rape. In fact, it already is rape; that's what he believes. Probably all he remembers about Todd Roark is that he was once spotted on a date with a white lady, not that Roark was canned for bouncing a check, which the cops called "kiting" because they had to get him on something and it had been eight years since antimiscegenation laws were ruled unconstitutional in California. Anyway, how do they know whether he had sex with her? He never said so, neither did she, and no one ever asked.

"Bet you don't get any white tail anymore, since you're not wearing that badge," Carpenter says, tapping the shield on his belt. "So you tried with that white lady, but she was too smart for you. Then you branched out for some dumb yellow pussy, too."

"You're nuts," Todd says, hoping that if this thing goes further they don't find out more about his life, none of it out of the ordinary, especially for cops, unless the cop isn't white. "You don't know what you're talking about." He says he was home, sleeping, on the nights of these crimes, re-covering from surgery for an ulcer in his eye.

"You'll have to prove that," Carpenter says. "And not one of your girlfriends."

Ah, that's what this is about—a big-dick contest, the one the white man is sure he'll lose, especially when the black man stands six-four. Pointing out that he gets plenty of tail without having to rape anyone doesn't help his cause here, so he has to come up with something else. He's scared but knows he better not sound it. Anger helps. He remembers how much crap he took from these crackers when he was one of Parker's boys.

"Then ask my pillow," Todd says. It's the wrong thing to say, the kind that regularly gets Negroes in custody a face full of knuckles. But he can take only so much; he's no Tom Bradley, the black sergeant he used to know, always careful to smile and bend over further no matter what's being rammed up there because he never knows when he might need the rammer. Tom—perfect name for him, Todd thinks. On the other hand, all black cops have to have a little Tom in them. It's the nature of the beast on Parker's force. Either you ride or get run over.

"I answered your questions, and I didn't do it, whatever you think I did," he says. "Feel free to check with my doctor to see I just had surgery. I'll give you his name. Now, can I go?"

"No."

"That means I'm under arrest?"

"Will be, once she nails your ass in the lineup."

"You know she's gonna do that? How?"

"She already picked you out once."

"Picked me out? Shit. The guy who raped her was pretending to be a cop, so you showed her my picture in uniform. Why'd you do that?"

"I didn't."

"Whoever. Why show her a picture of me at all? I'm no felon. I never raped nobody."

"Save it for the jury, pal."

Shit. This is one really bad dream. "My lawyer will be here soon."

John Marshall is there when the message Carpenter left for Steve finally gets to him, and Miko and Steve finally show up to view the lineup. Marshall likes to brag that he was named for the country's first chief justice, but any similarity ends there. Compared to him, Algonquin J. Calhoun on *Amos 'n' Andy* is Clarence Darrow.

Miko stares nervously but attentively through the one-way mirror at the six black men. She wants to be careful, is taking her time, and can't be sure.

Carpenter tells her that number four is the one she picked out in the photo. "Oh," she says. Marshall says nothing about the protocol violation.

Carpenter hands Miko the photo and says, "See." Marshall says nothing.

Miko studies Todd Roark and then the photo, Roark and the photo, Roark and the photo. She says his skin looks darker in the photo than it does in person.

Carpenter asks whether the rapist was light or dark. Dark, she says. Carpenter says maybe the bright lighting in the room makes number four look lighter. Marshall still says nothing.

Miko says, well, the other men, under the same lights, look darker than number four does. Carpenter says maybe she thought the rapist was darker than he really is because it happened in the dark, at night.

Maybe. "Number four," Miko announces.

Steve agrees.

Marshall says nothing.

His client is arrested.

CHAPTER TWENTY

Danny Galindo looked more surprised when he heard of Todd Roark's arrest than Todd Roark had when he was arrested. Roark, at least, had had some warning.

Danny, on the other hand, was down in the LAPD's public information office, hoping one of the officers would agree to direct the composites of the rapist to the white newspapers in town. They have to be convinced—the PI officers, not the editors—and it's no sure thing getting them to play ball, not the way it used to be when he knew the three main cops there pretty well. The three were more writers than cops, ghostwriting Parker's speeches and keeping their eyes out for stories they could sell to TV, just like Danny, the difference being that they were hoping to make a career of writing and Danny was there for the fun and a little extra cash. Back in '50, he and Sergeant Gene Roddenberry had taken an after-hours writing class together at Universal-International, and as of last year Roddenberry had left the department and was selling scripts full-time to shows like *Mr. District Attorney* and *Highway Patrol*. Same with Don Ingalls, about to go from story editor to producer, and Albert Germann, off to teach criminology at Michigan State. Now Danny hardly recognized the guys working PI, their number one job being to make Chief Parker's force look good, and so he needed to persuade them if he could to send out the rapist's composite; just asking wouldn't get it done.

"First off," the guy Danny talked to said, "no way any of the white papers runs this."

"You sure?" *Looks like Carpenter was right.*

"Too violent."

"Too violent?" That's a good one, Danny thought. This is L.A. How many times has he seen newspaper photos of detectives in their overcoats and fedoras standing over bullet-riddled corpses lying facedown in the L.A. River? That's what the members of the Gangster Squad, the cops trying to make sure that the city doesn't become Chicago west, live for. But maybe organized-crime bodies are different.

"Listen, every one of their crime reporters reads the blotter every night. They know what's going on in Darkville, and their editors don't want to hear it. How many stories you see in the *Times* or *Herald-Express* about cases you work down there?"

"True enough," Danny says. "But this is different."

"Why, because it's happening in the white parts of town?"

"Yeah. We want to alert people—keep 'em from getting hurt. And get their help catching him. These are kids it's happening to."

"Use your imagination, Detective. White readers, black rapist, panic in the streets, maybe even a race war, vigilantes prowling the night. I don't think it plays the way you're saying. Not even if they think this is another Caryl Chessman. At least Chessman is white."

"That'll sell a lot of papers, won't it?" Danny asked, thinking that the guy believed he was speaking for all Angelenos based on how he himself would react.

"But it's not good for business. Doesn't matter how many papers you sell if what you're writing makes people leave or newcomers not come in the first place. The owners of these papers, from the *Times* on down, the Chandlers, the Hearsts, they own plenty of real estate. And real estate needs customers, and customers spend a lot more on real estate than they ever do on newspapers."

Danny starts to argue a little, trying to convince him to at least pitch the editors on running the sketch—even without describing the crimes— when the guy interrupts, "I take it you didn't hear the news."

"Hear what?"

"We made a collar on this case."

"When? Who?"

"Todd Roark. Used to be a cop."

Roark? Really? Did he hear right? Yeah, Todd Roark.

Danny Galindo doesn't know whether to laugh or scream. He does not believe Todd Roark is their rapist. He believes the bad guy's out there. How does he know? He doesn't, not for sure. It's a gut feeling— and that shit-detecting gut is one of his best assets as a detective; rarely lets him down or leads him astray, as the facts attest later. He knows Roark a little, and Roark doesn't seem the type to pull this off or even to want to. They once ran into each other at the Olympic for fight night when Roark was a cop, even knocked back a few beers and had supper afterward at a rib joint off Central, where white cops wouldn't see them together and wonder about either of them. They both knew without saying a word it was something they had to do, having to drive east and south, each in his own car, before chowing down. But it was Roark who said it aloud.

Which was why, at the time, Danny couldn't understand Roark's carelessness taking a white lady to a restaurant in Hollywood where anyone could see them. Did he want to get caught? Maybe. (Yeah, *caught* is a strange word for something like that, and Danny doesn't like even thinking that way because it only endorses bigotry, but things are the way they are, and there's no use pissing and moaning about it, so *caught* is the right word.)

Danny doesn't know what he'd do himself if he were stuck working a traffic assignment for years straight with little hope of ever getting out, unless it was to go bang heads in the neighborhood where he lived. Anyway, when Roark was getting canned, Danny told him he thought he'd been forced into a raw deal and suggested he get a private dick's license. He said he thought Roark would do well—certainly better than he was allowed to do as a cop.

"The sketches don't look that much like him," Danny tells Carpenter.

Carpenter doesn't want to hear it:

"Case closed." It's his case. No point in Danny's saying that he's checked and Todd Roark doesn't own a car and has never registered a DeSoto, and no DeSoto that matches the description has been reported stolen. Neither does he bring up Caryl Chessman, though he knows it's what's on Carpenter's mind. The seventeen-year-old girl he abused identified Chessman, and she was farther from his face than this Japanese woman, who had to stare at the man who was ruining her. Or did she close her eyes the whole time?

Danny and Carpenter walk into Roark's arraignment in municipal court across the street from police administration and take seats at the back, waiting for the docket number to be read and Roark to be led in. Normally the detectives wouldn't show up for this and waste the city's money, but Carpenter is vested, wants to be sure the deputy district attorney asks for enough bail—and might even stand up and protest if the judge doesn't play along, risking a contempt of court.

By arrangement, the DA is now filing only kidnapping and assault charges against Roark, not rape, because Parker and the mayor and the city fathers selling all that real estate wouldn't want to read stories about one of their former cops, even if he is black, suspected of violating women across color lines; filed this way, there's no reason for reporters to pick up the story of just another Negro committing just another crime. All the police have to do now is keep the guy off the street, and only when they're sure that Roark's going down will they add the rape charge along with an explanation that'll make the department look good. With the new charges, he'll be entitled to a date in the gas chamber.

Before Roark's number is called, a procession of half a dozen idiots and their public defenders in five-buck suits are led in for their arraignments. They were arrested for mostly petty-ass shit like shoplifting a portable TV (without having a way to get it home fast—like a waiting car—once the moron carried it outside), or stealing a blank check, making it out to cash for a million bucks, and trying to cash it at a bank. Good thing for civilization's sake that most criminals are so stupid they pretty much arrest themselves.

Danny has been looking over the visitors' gallery, studying the people who stay as each defendant comes and goes. He wants to see if Roark has anyone in his corner and wonders if the black woman, midfifties, next to a black man the same age next to a pretty black girl of about twenty-three—none of them talking or commenting on the defendants or even looking at each other—are connected to Roark. The older woman, wearing a floral-print dress, has big features, like Roark, and the man next to her is light-skinned like Roark. The young woman wears a tight chiffon dress. Are they there for Roark? Danny gets his answer when the bailiff calls Roark's case number and leads him into the courtroom. At the sight of Todd Roark in handcuffs, the young woman gasps and covers her mouth with both hands. The older woman murmurs, "Lord Jesus." Danny figures they're his parents and new girlfriend.

Roark, with Marshall at his left elbow, steps to the bar and looks back at them over his right shoulder. He forces a thin smile, turns to the judge, pleads not guilty, sounding emphatic but depressed. Danny wonders whether he's been punched in the gut a few times. Of course, this whole thing's a gut punch.

Carpenter leans forward when the judge asks the deputy DA how much bail he wants, then looks satisfied and leans back when the DDA alludes to the callousness of these crimes and suggests $25,000.

Marshall protests that his client has no record and strong ties to the community—but smartly doesn't point out that Roark used to be a cop; if that became public, it would back the judge into making an example of him, especially because he's black. The judge settles on five grand, which is still a lot of money.

"Unless Roark's got a rich angel somewhere," Carpenter mutters to Danny, "he ain't getting out. No bondsman will take ten percent on this guy."

Carpenter, knowing what he's doing, stands as Roark is led away to draw Roark's attention so Roark can see his grin. It works. But Roark also spots Danny next to him. Surprise.

Danny's not looking at him, though. He's watching Roark's people. They're standing to leave. Holy shit. The mother rises—and keeps rising, like one of those inflatable bop-it clowns that get taller the more air you blow in. By the time the lady fully unfolds, he guesses she's a good six-three—about as tall as Roark. But the father, if that really is his father, isn't more than five-seven. So maybe it's not his father. Maybe it's his uncle. But on whose side?

Todd Roark spends a long three days in the city jail before he makes bail.

It took that long for all the paperwork. Julia Roark couldn't find a bail bondsman to accept five hundred bucks against the five grand, not without the deed to her house as collateral. So as long as she had to put up the house anyway—which they were all surprised to hear she's owned outright since 1949—she figured she might as well save the five hundred and just bring the deed to the county. Now, in the event Julia's son skips town before his trial, she'll be turned into the street—and he'll be hunted down by every cop in America. "I ain't worried," she told the clerk who'd insisted on spelling out the consequences. "I ain't scared."

"I can see that," he said, beholding this giant of a woman whose face says that you don't know the half of it.

CHAPTER TWENTY-ONE

Carpenter isn't happy about Roark's making bail, but not for the same reason Danny isn't happy. Danny understands that if the rapist pulls off another one while Roark is out—and of course the rapist is going to pull off another one; those guys always do—there won't be a cop who thinks it was only coincidence. Which means Danny won't be able to persuade the cops and the DA that they've got the wrong guy behind bars. Anyway, Roark won't be behind bars again until the cops rearrest him, and if they have to do that, Roark is going to pay. There might not be much of him left to put back behind bars.

All Danny can do is his job and let the rest happen. That Carpenter believes without question in Roark's guilt, and everything else is a waste of time, means Danny has to work this alone, preferably without anyone knowing. Danny wouldn't be surprised if somehow Carpenter is tailing Roark. Of course, that might be a good thing, because the rapist might do what he does at a time when Carpenter has his eye on Roark, and then he'd know the truth. Of course, whether he's actually willing to say the truth, that could be another matter. In any event, it's Danny's game now, and he's the only one who knows it.

Where to start?

Only one place: with the young lady who wasn't raped but spent ten minutes sitting beside him. Danny peeks at Margaret Bollinger's statement, memorizes everything she and her gentleman friend related and swore to. Her boardinghouse is at 1325 Ingraham, not far from there, not far from the place where the bad guy picked them up.

Margaret's landlady opens the door. Danny shows his badge, identifies himself as a police detective, and asks for Margaret Bollinger, which shocks the hell out of the landlady because Margaret hadn't told her anything about the encounter. Danny can see this whole story being written on the woman's face and immediately volunteers that Margaret's not in any trouble, hasn't committed any crime, but may have seen something that can help him with a serious investigation. Mollified but now more curious than ever, the woman ushers Danny into the parlor and tells him to sit on the couch. Danny stands.

He's in a good position to see Margaret when she comes down the stairs. And he hopes *his* whole story isn't written on his face, too. For some reason, it didn't occur to him that she'd be—well, that she was pretty. More than pretty. Very pretty. But more than that. His type. Funny, until this moment, he didn't know he had a type.

He says, "Miss Bollinger," showing his shield again. "I'm Detective Daniel Galindo."

"How do you do?" Her smile is the kind that can make you smile against your will, the kind that says you've been in the wrong place the last ten, fifteen years—maybe your whole life. It says you should live someplace where people have learned to smile just like that. Because it's sure not here. Here is a place where a young lady getting raped in a parking lot can cry out to a passerby to help her, and the rapist says, hey, come on, pal, don't ruin it for me, so the passerby passes by. This is a place where a young lady left in the bushes after being raped in Mac-Arthur Park can call out for help to a man walking by—and he'll rape her, too.

"I'm fine, thank you. And you?"

"Fine."

Stupid small talk. He can't believe he's doing it.

The landlady, more nosy than suspicious, butts in, "Detective Galindo wants to talk to you about an investigation."

"Yes," he says, "do you mind if I ask you a few questions?"

"Why don't you two sit down and I'll bring you some coffee," the landlady says, no doubt wondering why her boarder isn't asking what this matter is all about—and no doubt suspecting that she knows exactly what it's all about.

Danny doesn't want to talk there and can see that Margaret Bollinger also prefers to be out of earshot.

"Go ahead, Margie. Sit down."

Ah, she's called Margie. Danny was wondering if maybe she was Maggie. "Actually," Danny says, "I need Miss Bollinger to escort me somewhere. We won't be long." What? Why'd he explain that? This lady's not Margie's mother. He's not on a date. Or is he? He'd better not be. Right now he's so discombobulated, he has to remind himself to get a grip. Cops who even think about romance with victims or witnesses are canned faster than they can clean out their lockers. Imagine a guilty guy going free because some clever defense attorney lays out for the jury how the cop and the so-called victim concocted this whole story.

"I'll go grab my sweater," Margie says. She runs upstairs, leaving Danny and the landlady to each other.

"Do you have a gun?" the landlady asks.

"All policemen have guns," he says. "It's the law. Even when we're off duty, we're required to carry them."

"Good," she says.

Danny is puzzling over why she asked him—and why he answered—when Margie comes back down.

"Good night," she calls, leading Danny out. He holds the door, nodding to the landlady. He doesn't have to be uncomfortable. He's a cop, doing his duty.

Margie follows him down the steps, onto the sidewalk, toward the right.

Danny waits until he's sure the landlady isn't behind them and says, "Listen, last time someone showed you a badge and asked you to get in a car with him, he was lying about who he was. I just want you to be sure that you know that I am who I say I am. Here"—he holds it out—"take it, look at it." It's summer, so there's still enough daylight to make out all the grooves.

"Detective Galindo, I believe you."

"Don't believe me. Check for yourself."

Margie stares at it, or pretends to, and hands the shield back.

"I believe you," she says.

"I'd like you to accompany me somewhere."

"To the station? Again?"

"No, somewhere else."

"Where?"

"To meet someone."

"Do I have a choice?"

"Yes, you have a choice. You do *not* have to go. I can't make you go anywhere you don't want to go. This isn't a trick. There's just someone I want you to meet—if you can trust me, and I understand if you can't."

"Who?" she asks.

Danny doesn't answer; can't answer, she can see on his face.

"Okay," she says. "Let's go."

"Thank you."

He opens the passenger door of his late-model Ford—not his own car, the department's unmarked issue. Margie climbs in, he goes around the other side, and they drive off. There's silence for a while, only because he can't think of anything he wants to say. They listen to the voice of the female dispatcher over the radio, talking to other units. It's a thick silence. Margie finally asks where they're going because she recognizes her surroundings and doesn't like what she sees. They're at the end of Ingraham, where it meets Valencia—where she was with Charles Barker that night. In his periphery, Danny catches Margie tensing before he makes the left. She relaxes as he turns south, and she watches out the window.

"Do you own a car?" he asks.

"No."

"So this must all be new to you then?"

"Yes. Such an interesting city."

Interesting. Yeah, interesting. The perfect word. Interesting doesn't have to be good or bad. It is what it is. It's interesting. Never a dull moment.

He asks how long she's been here (a few months), and from where (rural Washington), and why she came to Los Angeles (change of pace), and what she plans to do (see the world before settling down), and whether she's working (temporary office job), and, all things considered, what she thinks of Los Angeles so far (exciting, to say the least).

Then comes the money question. "How's your boyfriend feel about what happened to you two?"

"Charles? He's not my boyfriend."

Bingo.

"Oh?"

"We were set up on a blind date."

"So how's he doing?"

"I don't know."

"Oh."

"I haven't seen him since that night."

That's great news. But it shouldn't be. He doesn't want it to be. He doesn't want to want it to be. He doesn't want to care. He's wondering how he can stop himself.

"Oh," he says.

Danny makes a series of turns in a quiet residential area, small lawns, pulling to the curb in front of a house with a porch out front. It's twilight. Already a light's on inside, visible through the curtain.

"Is this where we're going?" she asks.

"Yes," he says, getting out. He comes around and opens her door, helps her to her feet, leads her to the porch but doesn't let her get in front of him. He's more nervous than he thought he'd be, and turning a little away from her, he quickly checks the revolver in his shoulder holster beneath his sport jacket. He unbuttons the jacket, steps to her right side so that, if he has to, he can reach the gun quickly without putting her in a line of fire.

He knocks on the door.

A light comes on the porch.

Heavy footsteps from inside.

The door swings open.

There stands a large, light-skinned black man wearing a who-the-hell-is-it-what-do-you-want look. Just like that, though, Todd Roark recognizes Danny Galindo—but not Margie Bollinger.

Even before Danny says hello, even before he lets his right hand that's been on gun alert relax, he has watched how both Todd and Margie regard each other.

They've never seen each other. He now knows that for sure. He was right: they arrested the wrong guy. Even better, Margie doesn't hold what happened to her against all Negroes.

"Danny," Roark says.

"Todd."

This is a surprise, Roark says.

Yeah, says Danny. How you doing?

Roark exaggeratedly blows a lungful of air out his lips and with his eyes says, *Do you really have to ask?*

"You coming in?" Roark pushes the screen open.

Danny maneuvers Margie in front of him, then changes his mind and guides her with his hand back to his side. "Ah, no, better not. I have to get her home. I'll give you a call."

"Okay."

Danny takes Margie's elbow and leads her down the three steps to the concrete sidewalk.

"Danny," Roark calls, "thanks."

Without looking back, Danny raises his hand, then opens the car door for Margie.

On the way, she asks what that was about, though she can guess.

"Did he look familiar to you?" Danny asks, obliged professionally to phrase the question as a question instead of as confirmation of his impression that they'd never seen each other.

"No."

"I didn't think so."

"Is that the man you think—"

"No."

"But someone else does?"

"Yeah."

"Who?"

"Pretty much the whole police department and district attorney."

"Oh. So does me not recognizing him mean he won't be arrested?"

"Already was. He's out on bail."

"For what he did to me? But he—"

"No, for what happened to someone else."

"There's someone else?"

"You were lucky, Margie. Very, very lucky." Pause. "She was raped."

Damn, he shouldn't have told her that. He just couldn't help himself. He'll take her home now.

And he won't see her again unless he has to. Unless it's strictly business.

Yeah, right.

CHAPTER TWENTY-TWO

Sometimes Willie Fields thinks his head is exploding. He can't quite figure out what's what. Yesterday was Friday. At ten in the morning a loud siren from somewhere miles away started blaring in waves that sounded like crying. Not a cop car or fire truck. Shit. The Russians. They finally dropped the big one. The end of the world any minute.

He jumped down off the ladder and began running around like a decapitated chicken and whooping like a banshee, looking for a place to hide from the blast. The other guys were laughing their asses off and pointing at him till someone finally took pity and told him it was a monthly test of the warning system just in case the Big One ever does come; it didn't mean anything; it had gone off the previous month—remember?—and would go off next month, too.

Fields pretended not to be embarrassed. It wasn't hard to pretend because he wasn't embarrassed. How was he supposed to remember all that about when something's real and when it isn't? What happens if they drop the big one on Friday at ten, huh?

Now the guys felt a little bad for ragging on him yet again. To let him have a little dignity, they purposely got to talking about backyard bomb shelters, making it seem that he wasn't so stupid for being a scaredy-cat. But they can't quite manage to keep the talk serious. Blue is the only one who owns his own house, so he's the only one who could build a shelter, and he said, I wouldn't want any of you bums in there with me and my wife, and I don't want to be the only one left in the world if the only other person left with me is my old lady. The guys roared. Not Willie Fields. How come? They were trying to involve him now and asked what he thought he'd need to survive in a bomb shelter till it was safe to come out, and about six guys at the same time answered for him, "Pussy!"

"Course," said Darryl, "ain't enough stone foxes in all L.A. to keep him good and busy next forty years."

Fields is, after all, according to his own calculations, which they find credible, the man who's already gotten it on with about five hundred ladies since he first got it on at age twelve.

Fields wasn't paying attention, even though they were talking about him in the way they thought he liked being talked about. He'd already moved on, if he'd even been there in the first place. They didn't know that. They thought he was pissed and pouting, his feelings hurt, this big, good-natured guy, a life-size old teddy bear, dumb as soap. So what if he'd fuck mud?

Aloysius, the oldest of the bunch, who never met a man he didn't like and had a son going off to college soon, put an arm on Fields's back, saying not to fret, "We don't mean nothin' by it, Willie," and after looking over at the others for the go-ahead, mentioned how they were planning a drive down to Anaheim Sunday to go see that new Disneyland place. "We ain't sure we can get in," he said. "Might not be integrated. But I hear you can see a big mountain they built even if you can't get in. They got a hotel cross the street that just opened, too, could go check that out, too. Cost ten million smackers to build. Must be somethin', yeah?

Try having a drink there, and if that don't work out, maybe they let us in to Knott's Berry Farm—s'posed to be the best damn fried chicken this side the Mississippi. Whaddya say, Willie? Whyn't you come with?"

Fields didn't respond, didn't even look at him, because he didn't care anymore anyway. He was far away, wondering what Friday night might hold at the Keyhole Lounge on South Western, where Dudley Brook was tinkling the ivories now.

But Dudley Brook or no Dudley Brook, Friday night turned out not to hold anything, and he was a little down when he woke with that feeling like some bomb's about to go off in his forehead.

It's not pain, exactly, it's more like air inside a balloon getting bigger and still empty. Could pop any second. So he turns on the TV and sits in bed and watches *Sky King,* the show about the West that has a plane instead of a horse. Basically, it's *Fury* in the sky. He's seen this episode before, a few months ago, but can't remember how it turns out. Sky and Penny and Bob use the plane to rescue some men from a huge flood in a canyon, but the men are actually bad guys who force Sky and Penny and Bob into helping them rob a bank that got flooded. All ends happily, though, and now Fields is hungry.

He fills a bowl with Frosted Flakes and grabs some milk out of the icebox. He knows he's supposed to call it a fridge, but old habits die hard. As soon as he opens the bottle top, he can smell the sour. That's what happens after a couple of weeks. So does he use water or eat the cereal dry? Wait a second. Yeah. Hamm's. He's got half a can left. It may be flat but it's cold and not sour. Not bad, actually. You know why? 'Cause Hamm's is from the land of sky-blue waters.

Willie Roscoe Fields considers himself an expert on ad campaigns. He takes them seriously, thinking hard and sometimes long about them. For instance, he uses Pepsodent toothpaste and wonders where the yellow went. He doesn't smoke Chesterfields, he smokes Kools—'cause he loves the cool menthol—but he's still planning on someday buying a pack of Chesterfields to see if it's true that there's "not a cough in the pack." And then there's Wonder bread; it "builds strong bodies twelve ways"— except he still can't figure out more than three of them. Oh, and "Does she or doesn't she? Only her hairdresser knows for sure." Well, Fields is pretty goddamn sure she does, or at least wants to—and if she doesn't, he'd sure like to be the one who does her first.

He gets in the car just to get in it, doesn't care where he's going, anywhere but here. He's got a whole day to kill before tonight's festivities. He chooses west, down Pico. And for a second he wishes he'd gone with the guys from work to Disneyland. Or is that on Sunday?

Then the radio comes on, the last syllable or two of Ol' H.H., leading right into a commercial for L&M cigarettes that makes him reach for his Kools and push in the lighter. He knows every word of the ad, just like it's a song, and says it along with the pro, just like he's singing: "They say you couldn't make a cigarette with such exciting taste in such an improved filter. But L&M did it. Puff by puff, today's L&M gives you less tars and more taste." He even does the echo effect, dropping his voice an octave, making it sound like God himself: "Less tars, more taste." What he doesn't do is sing along with the jingle that ends the ad, crooned by a bunch of white kids who sound like they're smiling and wearing bow ties with blue sport coats and taking craps that don't stink and saying "Golly gee whiz and willickers, Mom" when she lays out cookies and milk after school: "Light into that L&M flavor. You're really livin' when you do."

"Yeah," says Fields, punctuating the jingle with an exclamation point before lighting the cigarette and inhaling deeply.

"Good huntin' with Hunter Hancock," says the disc jockey. "Ol' H.H. on the fabulous KPOP, your home for rhythm and blues. We got the rhythm so you don't get the blues. Your weather for today, Angelenos? Same as yesterday, same as tomorrow and the day after that: late-night and morning low clouds and local fog extending inland along the coast.

High today in the city, eighty-four; low tonight, sixty-eight. You can add another ten degrees in the valleys, where it's smokin' hot"—and behind his voice comes the intro of "Fever"—"but not as hot as this young man. Here's the pride of Detroit, Little Willie John. Lord almighty, he's got the fever. And he's burning up the charts."

This is the best song ever, sung and played better than any song ever—just enough, not too many instruments—and Fields can never believe it's on the radio. Don't all those Goody Two-shoes realize it's about fucking and nothing more, sung at the rhythm that ladies like to be loved and he likes to love them? Come to think of it, they didn't know that about "Sixty Minute Man" either. Little Willie sings, "Never know how much I love you, never know how much I care. When you put your arms around me, I get a fever that's so hard to bear. You give me fever."

Fields is torn between singing along, which he can do fine, and just listening, so he just listens. But not just. Snapping his fingers with Little Willie's, his other hand pounds the steering wheel in time with his head, his shoulders, his hips, even his dick—man, the backbeat is a Spanish fly. If he could, he'd play this song again and again and again, play it whenever he's making time with a lady, even when there's no lady around and he does himself before getting the blue balls so bad he can hardly walk. "When you put your arms around me, I get a fever that's so hard to bear." Again and again and again. "Take these arms I'll never use and believe what my lips have to say." Fields looks in the rearview mirror and watches himself kiss the air. Oh, mama.

"That's Little Willie John on King Records," says Ol' H.H., "and you can buy it for your own down at Dolphin Records in both seventy-eight rpm, and"—he drags the word out—"forty-five rpm, too, in case you've got one of those new record players in your living room."

Fields doesn't have a record player, new or old, in his living room—doesn't even have a living room. But maybe he'll get one and play that song again and again and again. He's so hot right now when he pulls into the Texaco station on La Brea, he doesn't hear the ding his tires make on the black driveway signal hose, so it's a surprise when the guy in the starched uniform, the little army private's hat looking stupid on his head, leans down.

"Fill 'er up, sir?" he asks.

"Ethyl," Willie says. Maybe the high-octane will turn his DeSoto into one of those 265 V-8 'Vettes. He turns off the engine but the radio stays on.

What a crappy mood he's in. Sweaty, too. He leans over to crank down the passenger window. Still no breeze. The attendant puts the hose in the tank before spraying the windshield from his little bottle and wiping with paper towels. Fields remembers when he used to do that job. Hated it.

"And speaking of King and records," says Ol' H.H., "I'm still getting letters from a lot of you who were at that rally in support of the Montgomery, Alabama, bus boycotters a few weeks ago at Jefferson High School, where the Reverend Martin Luther King spoke about what he and his Southern Christian Leadership Foundation are trying to accomplish—and apparently *are* accomplishing. He said, and I quote, 'We must not become overoptimistic with the probability that the end is in sight and that the forces at work will bring the era of justice and brotherhood to bear. We cannot sit idly by and await the new. We must fight now for what we are to have and meet the challenges that face us.'"

Fields knows Ol' H.H. is reading what someone said. Sounds to him like a sermon, and he can't remember the last one he heard. Turns out he's no better now at understanding them than he was then, standing in church, waiting for the choir's turn again. "Unfortunately," Ol' H.H. says, "I wasn't there to hear Mr. King, so I don't know that they played music. Oh, gospel, I'm sure, but for something new, I think this would've been fitting."

Gogi Grant singing "The Wayward Wind." It's "a restless wind," she says. Damn song's played twice an hour on every station. Why can't they do that with "Fever" instead? That's hardly ever on. *And what the fuck is a wayward?*

Pissed, Fields turns off the radio. This fill-up's sure taking a long time. He glances at the pump. So far only ten gallons in.

Across the street a big billboard ad for that Madman Muntz catches his eye—Muntz wearing that crazy outfit, eyes bugged out, mouth wide-open, pretending to say, "You look terrible behind that wheel." Damn, Fields knows Muntz wants to sell him a car, just like he sold him that TV; and he knows that Muntz can't really see him from up there. Just the same, he wonders if he really does look bad behind the wheel. It's something to think about. Fields remembers that guy who figured him for a Caddy driver, and the Caddy he tried to buy over the phone.

On the other side of Tenth is another billboard, this one for the LAPD. "A great city deserves a great force. Join now." And it gives a number to call. The idea worms into his brain. He thinks about it. Then he thinks about how much he should think about it. Not much, he decides.

The attendant lifts the hood and checks the oil, bringing the dipstick around to show him that it's all right, but Fields waves him off. He's still staring at the billboard when he hears the hose click full at $3.16. The guy slams the hood and asks if Fields wants the tires checked. No. Fields just wants out of there.

The attendant squeezes four cents more gas in, hangs the hose on the pump, and says, "That'll be three-twenty," glancing back at the pump to make sure he remembered right.

Fields counts out the money, and the guys asks, "You want Green Stamps or Blue Chip?"

Fields laughs. "Hell, no." Bullshit trading stamps. He once filled a book with all the little empty squares where the stamps go, leaving a bad taste on his tongue—took him months to buy enough stuff to get enough stamps to paste them sort of neatly inside—and brought it to the redemption center, thinking he'd get himself a radio. But for something like that, the lady told him, you need about fifty books.

Fields hands the attendant three dollar bills and a quarter, says, "Keep the change," and drives off. Nice to leave the brother a little tip.

He's heading north on La Brea and has to stop for the light at Wilshire. He likes this part of town; feels he can breathe there. A new, green Thunderbird pulls up next to him, two young guys inside with crew cuts, their windows down and radio up loud, "Don't Be Cruel" getting his attention, but he can't be obvious about looking over; can't let them see him looking, can't call out and tell them how much he digs their wheels. But he does. Should be him driving that thing.

When the song ends, a man's professional voice says, "Here are some most happy fellas, the Four Lads for Ford." And now their song. He looks at the guys in the Thunderbird. The way they look, and how the song sounds, wouldn't surprise him if they're two of the four lads. "Standing on the corner watching all the Fords, standing on the corner giving all the boys the eye. Thunderbird's kissing cousin."

The light turns green, the Thunderbird patches out, and suddenly Fields hates his DeSoto.

It's still early, three o'clock. Plenty of time to waste before tonight. He'll stop at Pink's on La Brea and Melrose for a couple of chili dogs, then cruise up to Hollywood Boulevard, park, see what's playing at some of those theaters along the street, pick one, watch a movie, doesn't matter what, get his mind off his troubles. Which is what he does, settling on the movie with the best poster art in the marquee, the one with that dragon-looking thing blowing yellow fire. He remembers that some guys at work saw this one, said it scared the shit out of them. *Godzilla, King of the Monsters*. "Incredible, unstoppable, titan of terror," the poster says. "Civilization crumbles as its death rays blast a city of 6 million from the face of the earth."

Fields buys a Bit-O-Honey and in the dark finds a seat off to the side, alone. There's about ten minutes left of the other picture, *She-Creature*. He hates that the beautiful woman becomes a creature instead of the creature becoming a beautiful woman. When the lights come up, he sees the theater half-filled, most of them kids. He looks down, pretending to be reading the Bit-O-Honey wrapper so that no one looks directly at him, and he tells himself he doesn't have to take a piss when really he does. Finally *Godzilla* starts. It's pretty good right from the beginning, enough to keep him from getting up to piss. One character says, "If we do not defend ourselves from Godzilla now, what will become of us?" So the doctor says, "And what will become of us if a weapon such as I have now falls into the wrong hands?" *Then you're fucked,* Fields thinks. "You have your fear, which *might* become reality," the first man says in that Jappo accent. "And you have Godzilla, which *is* reality." Fields thinks he understands that, but why do they have to do all that talking before getting to the monster? Just show the thing and blow it to hell already, because you're gonna do it anyway, so what the fuck? If you only showed the good parts, you could make the movie twenty minutes and charge a nickel instead of half a buck.

Fields stays and sits through *She-Creature,* so he can see her looking beautiful, until the part where he came in the first time. Now he can sneak out in the dark and take that piss without people seeing him, and it's late enough to go do what he has to do. First, though, he stops for two more chili dogs at Pink's, and this time doesn't have the guy put on any onions because he doesn't want his breath to smell when he pulls up behind the Rambler just off Larchmont, takes the young man for a short ride before pushing him out, and in the backseat treats the cute blonde to what he's sure is the best fifteen minutes of her life.

Even if he does have to keep his hand clasped over her mouth to keep her from screaming.

Even if, at the police station later—and for months afterward—she runs every few minutes to the toilet, feeling like he's still leaking out of her.

CHAPTER TWENTY-THREE

Julia Roark is sixty-nine years old. She follows the story of Caryl Chessman, whom she calls an "evil, evil man." She knows that her son Todd is in serious trouble for something he didn't do. And every morning and every night she prays harder for him than she did during those two years he was fighting in the Philippines with Jap bullets flying around his head.

Todd's leaning back in her living room's big easy chair, chin in the air, holding a little blue cup (it came in the box) filled with collyrium over the bad eye, the one with the ulcer in it that hurts like hell. If he has to go back to jail—and unless they catch the bad guy in the act the next time he rapes someone, he's almost surely going back—there's no way they'll let him bring the stuff with him. He may not even have an eye left anyway. That's why he's a little upset that Mom bailed him out. As glad as he is to be free, he's not really free now. He may be worse off. No, he's definitely worse off, starting the second the next victim reports the crime. Or even if she doesn't; even if the guy gives up raping. Guess who takes the fall? He may never be really free again.

The Johnny Otis Show is on the DuMont TV and they're trying to watch, but a few days ago the story broke that one of the show's regular singers, Charles Tiger, a member of the Premiers, was busted for fucking a thirteen-year-old. He's eighteen. That's a crime—if they can make it stick. Even if they don't, that's all people will remember about him. And look at Otis as he stands there with the remaining Premiers, like he smells a fart and doesn't want it in his nose or on his jacket.

No matter what, this is going to be what happens to Todd, too. He and Julia both know it.

It's going to be bad when that Japanese lady takes the stand to say what happened to her, and the prosecutor mentions how close Roark came a dozen times to being slaughtered by the Japs during the war and how often he saw or heard about how unbelievably sadistic the Japs were to the Filipinos—for instance the way they'd sometimes stuff a hundred priests and nuns into a space big enough for twenty and then seal the windows and doors, and when the bodies were decomposing and giving off gases, any spark would send the place kablooey. So he's got some payback in him he'd like to pay back, they'll say.

It's going to be bad when the jury hears that he had to marry a teenage Filipina he knocked up, and that after the war he left her and the boy behind. The boy's name is Floyd. He's poor, and being mixed black makes it that much harder on him back there—so Todd's got some added incentive, they'll say.

It won't look good when someone mentions—and someone will, you can count on that—why his wife Thelma divorced him while she was pregnant with their daughter. *She did it, listen up, everyone, when she caught him having an affair with the lady who's in the gallery right now.* Queenie's her name. She's an aspiring show-business entertainer, wink, wink. And you'll notice that neither Thelma nor her daughter Teri Denise is anywhere to be seen. In other words, ladies and gentlemen of the jury, this Negro you see before you just can't keep it zipped up, even when he knows the terrible cost to others and himself.

And, oh, he's got a violent streak—that'll come out, too. It'll come out how he and his sisters Hannah, Frances, Anna Mae, and Cleo were raised to argue and fight and compete over everything from where they sit to what plays on the radio, and how two of the sisters once went at Roark with a knife. It'll come out how his mother and father spent the thirty years of their marriage, before Dad went off to farm in Fresno, fighting and scrapping and shouting, the little five-seven guy standing up to the six-three lady with the size-thirteen shoe, making her so mad that once when they were still living in Texas she picked up a fireplace poker, the kind with a hook on the end, and took a vicious swing at him, but he leaned out of the way and the tip of the poker popped their daughter Cleo square in the eye—turned it to jelly.

The good stuff about him won't come out, like what an otherwise decent man Todd Roark is, that he was decorated for bravery in the war, was promoted to first lieutenant, and had the respect of his soldiers; or how he was raised in a purely God-fearing home believing there's good reason to fear God. Not counting how he likes the ladies and how the ladies seem to love him, which shouldn't be counted considering how many millions Dean Martin, for example, is piling up either doing the same thing or pretending to, Roark is about as decent a man as you'll find. He's so decent, in fact, that no way will he let Queenie take the stand to humiliate her unwed self by telling the truth, and the truth is that she can vouch for where he was on the nights he was supposedly raping those women; he was with her, in his bed, and just in case you were wondering, yes, she would've damn well smelled another woman on him no matter how her scent got there, if by some miracle he managed to sneak out of the house with the door right there after loving her long and hard three times in three hours and then doing what they say he did and then somehow sneaking back into bed without her waking up. Of course, to have done all that, he'd actually need a—what's the word?—car.

Queenie would do it, she'd tell them all that in open court. And do it proudly. When the time comes, she'll be begging to let him let her be his alibi, crying that his freedom and their future together are more important than whatever someone who doesn't know her thinks of her from what the prosecutor lied about in his opening statement. But Todd can't let her get up there on the stand and testify to all the dirty little details that she'd obviously have to tell the prosecutor, who obviously won't call her as a prosecution witness, knowing what she told the police. That's why he'll forbid his attorney to call her as a defense witness, so she can skate clear. It's bad enough the way people look at him now. He doesn't want that for her, too. He's done a lot in this world that he'd like to take back, and while this won't make up for it, at least he won't have something else to feel bad about when he's marking notches in the wall, one per day.

Anyway, what does it matter? Even a parade of saints, celebrities, and psychiatrists testifying that no man who does as well with women as Todd Roark does would ever resort to that kind of behavior will be a match for when the prosecutor calls an LAPD captain to hint at the reason Roark was really fired from being a cop.

That's the other bad thing about having been a cop. He's seen it over and over. Once he gets to court, the facts and logic stop mattering. Only the story matters. Only what the jury remembers of what they want to believe and already believed matters. Not the facts. Still, no way he's taking a plea deal to save himself from the gas chamber. Let them find him guilty. He's not going to do it for them.

Julia Roark is five feet away, in her best chair, the green floral one with the plastic protective covering, her long, sturdy legs reaching almost to the TV. She glances over at her son to see if this is a good time to tell him what she has to tell him about his daughter. It's not, but she has to say it anyway, and there's no hesitation or apology in her voice when she says, "I saw Teri Denise today."

This gets Todd's attention fast. He whips around, turning his good eye to her, and puts down the collyrium cup on the little table between them. "Where?"

"Here, she was here."

"Teri Denise was here today?"

"I watched her for a while."

"Thelma dropped her off?"

"Dropped her off. Ran some errands. Gone about two hours."

"She called you?"

"Yeah." Julia shrugs.

He stands, trying to process this. "She didn't call me."

Julia doesn't have to say anything now. She knows he knows Thelma's done calling him. Then something occurs to him: "You didn't call me either. I'da hopped right on the Normandie bus and come right over."

"Mm-hmm."

Now he's pacing. Todd has listened to that *mm-hmm* all his life and can't remember that it ever meant good news. *No use arguing with gravity* is what he hears when she says it. *Things are the way they are, and you sleep in the bed that you make. Maybe, just maybe, if you act right, you'll get your reward on the other side.* That's how she lives. She's done all right.

"She tell you not to call me?" he asks.

"She didn't have to."

Todd Roark grabs his pack of Salems off the TV; it's a new kind of cigarette, just introduced, a filter-tip menthol that someone with a big basketful was giving away on a street corner—two, three, four packs if you wanted. They're not bad. And they were free. He lights one and sits back down in the chair, shaking his head over how his ex-wife dropped his twenty-three-month-old daughter off at his mother's house, not his, while she ran to do whatever she needed to. There just ain't nothing to say about that, nothing that can make anything better.

"She's still my granddaughter," Julia says.

"And she's my daughter."

"Mm-hmm."

"So now you're her babysitter?"

"I hope so. Would be my pleasure. She's a fine child. Smart as a whip. Talking up a storm already."

"She coming back anytime soon?"

"I don't know. But I don't expect I'll see her all that much more."

"Why not?"

Julia pauses before coming straight out with it. "Thelma's moving."

"Somewhere the other side of town?"

"San Diego."

"Huh? San Diego? What the hell for, to get away from me? Cause of this? Lord Jesus, that's—"

"Son, she's getting married."

Todd absorbs the two-by-four, stubs the lit cigarette in the cup of collyrium, lets it fall to the table. He stands and steadies himself on the arms of the chair. The living room isn't wide enough to pace. The ceiling is too low to breathe.

Julia moves the wet butt from the cup into the ashtray. "The man's got a fine job down there," she says, standing tall enough to look him straight in the eye. "Engineer for one of the airplane companies. Already put a deposit payment on a new house in a nice, new area."

"He's white?" Todd asks.

"No, Negro."

"Mm-hmm." he says.

Todd Roark walks to the bus stop on Normandie, waits fifteen minutes for the ten-minute ride, and walks from the bus to his street. He gets close enough to his house to hear the phone ringing inside. It's his mom calling, trying to warn him that the cops were just there, looking for him. He won't get inside to answer it, though. Doesn't even make it to the front door before six of them come out of nowhere and tell him to put up his hands.

CHAPTER TWENTY-FOUR

Negroes don't all look alike to Danny Galindo, so he can't understand how some people make that mistake. But a mistake it is, even if this newest young rape victim and her scared young man telling the same story about a huge Negro with a badge and flashlight and knife both picked out Todd Roark's photo from an array and then pointed to him in the lineup, with maybe a little coaching from Carpenter. She was crying—sobbing, actually—but you could tell that if she had a razor blade and five seconds of opportunity, Roark would be missing his dick and have had four seconds to think about living without it before she slit his throat, too. Danny isn't sure Carpenter wouldn't have given her the blade. And the opportunity.

Carpenter has been taking plenty of bows and back pats for wrapping this up so fast, putting that dumbass nigger rapist away where he belongs. Might even win a commendation for it, if the brass doesn't think the ceremony and all will call too much attention to how Roark used to be a cop. Anyway, that's what some of the cops are whispering. Others think they should shout it out as a way of cleverly but just the same clearly telling Negroes that trying to join the LAPD might not be in their best interest—and sending the word to the fellows at the academy that maybe they could be a little more choosy about whom they let in.

Carpenter knows far beyond any shadow of a doubt that they've got their rapist, and he's going to convince the DA to insist on no bail and no plea for this scumbag. Probably won't be a problem—that is, unless Danny says something to someone with Margie Bollinger backing him up. Doing that would absolutely surprise hell out of Carpenter and also something a lot uglier than just surprise. As far as Carpenter's concerned, seeing no reason to think differently, Danny's with him all the way on this. Of course he is. Why wouldn't Danny be with him? What would possibly make Danny think that they hadn't gotten one more bad hombre off the street? No way he'd even spend a second wondering why or what.

For now, Danny wants it that way. There's always been a little mattress pea between Carpenter and Danny because Carpenter is older and wasn't in the war, didn't face the fires—and he can never get out of his mind the thought that Danny saw and did things that Carpenter can never live up to. So Danny has no common ground with him to build on besides policing itself. If he plays his doubts about Roark's guilt too soon, he won't have any credibility when the rapist hits again; won't be able to point out that Todd Roark couldn't very well have raped young Jane Doe while he was locked up in the L.A. City Jail. It would go something like this: *Hey, wait a second, Roark can't be two places at once. Maybe we got the wrong guy.* To which Carpenter might start thinking twice about his presumption and actually acknowledge that, you know, a few of the details just don't fit so well.

But if Danny has already said something to Carpenter, putting a wedge between them when Carpenter thinks Danny's got no good reason for skepticism—or, worse, he decides the reason is that Danny's brown and Roark's black and maybe shines and tacos stick up for each other—then it would go something like this: *You know, Roark can't be two places at once.* Followed by *Yeah, well, you didn't think he could be in* one *place.*

At some point, Carpenter's going to realize how wrong he is, and Danny doesn't have the least idea how he'll react—though it's hard to imagine he'll take it well. A detective can't detect if he's gone blind and stupid, and suddenly recognizing that you have totally fucked up this very big-deal case, even for a supposedly good reason, has just got to kick the shit out of you.

And when that moment happens, there might be others around; and the others will probably—definitely—have thought the same thing about Roark. They're going to have to come to Jesus, too. All of them eventually. Then what? If Danny had to bet, he'd lay one to one that fifty and a half percent of them won't thank him for making sure they haven't stepped in a puddle of steaming crap. That's okay. Danny isn't doing this to make friends. Not that he doesn't like being liked. He does. Just not more than he likes doing his job right. The funny part is that they think they get along with him, when really he's the one getting along with them.

Danny's bigger problem is that his mission isn't just to exonerate Todd Roark (which is at least possible, unlike rehabilitating his name; that's beyond anyone's power, because not even innocence washes away the stench, maybe ever). No, Danny's more urgent job right now is to keep the bad guy out there from ruining any more lives than he already has. That won't be easy, especially since he has to do it all by himself. And on the q.t.

Come to think of it, that's just not feasible either. The truth is that until the guy ruins at least one more life, Todd Roark is going to have to take the heat.

Which also means that if the rapist skips town or drives off a cliff or gets a knife in the belly at the Club Milomo some night before someone connects him to the crimes, Roark's going to be the one who pays for

them. Maybe with his life. California's version of the Little Lindbergh
Law says that any kidnapping that leads to bodily harm is eligible for the
death penalty. So now Danny starts hoping that the bad guy does strike
again, but that he picks out the wrong car—a Studebaker, say, with
someone in it like that marine Margie was with. Only this time the boyfriend is packing and not afraid to shoot and keep shooting until the
cylinder is empty. Being carted away by the coroner with the fake badge
in one hand and a flashlight in the other would solve a lot of problems—
and damn, wouldn't that be interesting, being in the car in a lovers' lane
that this guy tries to hit?

In the cell, Roark separates himself from the other five young men,
all of them Negroes, one of them taking a dump on the filthy porcelain
john; and it stinks all the way over here. Roark's big enough to command some respect with just a look, even though they know he was a
cop, which means he'll have to sleep with an eye open until they move
him to either his own cell or double accommodations. It'll have to be his
one good eye, because the bad one is red and swollen, getting worse.

"Back off," Danny says to the others in his don't-fuck-with-me way.

First he and Roark talk in normal voices. How you doing? Danny
asks.

How you think?

You okay?

Good as I'm gonna be.

Your eye doesn't look so good.

It's not.

Anything you need?

I think you know the answer to that.

Danny nods and leans in close, sticking his nose through the bars a slat to the left of where Roark does the same, except bending at the knees a little, so their mouths are next to each other's right ear.

"I can get you out," Danny whispers. "Today, if you want."

"That girl?"

"Yeah."

"Why'd you bring her by the house instead of when I was here last time?"

"You see a guy behind bars, it's easy to think he belongs there."

"And no one has to know what she saw."

"Yet."

"That's why I better stay put till you catch him. Even if I could make bail."

"I figured. But I wanted you to know. Just in case it gets bad in here."

"It's already bad." He doesn't say that the bruises are in places that don't show. "And it's gonna get worse if the real guy doesn't take my place. You alone on this?"

"So far."

"Any good leads?"

"Not so far."

Danny goes upstairs and before reaching the front door realizes that in a second, when he crosses the threshold, there won't be a single man in the building who doesn't want to see Todd Roark meet a bad end. And most would like to help him get there.

CHAPTER TWENTY-FIVE

JUDGE FINES GROUP DENIED SERVICE

CHICAGO—A Chicago judge in an astonishing verdict held that six members of an interracial group who had been refused service by a Southside café were guilty of disorderly conduct. He fined all of them $100 each.

Although one of the group was beaten up and police refused to arrest his attackers, Judge Alexander J. Napoli held that when the defendants insisted upon their rights, they created a risk that the restaurant owner would resort to violence against them. Therefore, they were guilty of disorderly conduct.

—An article that appeared in the *California Eagle* but not in any white newspaper— the *Los Angeles Times,* the *Herald-Express,* the *Examiner,* the *Mirror*—during the summer of 1956.

CHAPTER TWENTY-SIX

Willie Fields comes home, walks upstairs, picks up his mail, opens the door, and lifts the window to the backyard. He smells smoke. It's trash-burning time. Mrs. Terrell is sitting on a milk crate beside the incinerator, staring ahead and not at anything in particular, smoking a Winston. A closed shoebox is on her lap. She doesn't look like she's waiting to burn it.

He flips through the mail. Two envelopes. One's from his credit union. The other from PO Box 110, Venice, California. He doesn't recognize that. Oh, wait. That's right. One time when he was reading the *Eagle,* he saw a little ad that said, "Money, the Bible tells how to get it." To find out what the Bible tells, you were supposed to send a dollar to that post office box. It's been so long since he did—two weeks since he decided he'd been taken, and a week and a half since he forgot about it. But now here's the answer. He rips open the envelope and inside is a card. "Work hard. —So sayeth the Bible." That's all. Fields stares at it for a second, then lays it on the dresser. He'll deal with this later. He pours a drink, downs it, pours another.

Mrs. Terrell is still there, still staring straight ahead, still smoking. Maybe he'll go down, sit a spell, have a smoke with her, ask if she wants him to throw anything heavy in the incinerator. Sometimes Fields feels kindly toward his landlady and likes her company. That might have something to do with not wanting to fuck her. She's way too old. It's a relief for him, not wanting to. He leaves his drink, grabs his pack of Kools, and goes out back.

"Hey," he says.

She grunts a syllable without moving, and Fields sees how sad her face is. Short of crying, it's as sad as faces get. He hasn't seen her look that way. He just found out a while ago she's originally from New Orleans, too, but that was way back, twenty years. Anyway, she's had plenty of sad days, including coming home once and seeing her husband hanging out of the second-story window, all of him hanging out except his head, the window sash down on his neck. She found out later that he'd forgotten his key and climbed up knowing the upstairs window was closed but unlocked, and just when he'd balanced himself and pushed up the window, he had one of his epileptic fits and something happened to make the window slam down on his neck. They couldn't tell her how long he took to die, but at thirty she was a widow with nothing. So, yeah, she's cried before, and this may be one of those times.

"Mind if I smoke with you?" he asks.

"Uh-uh," she manages.

Is that a yes or a no? He'll take it as a yes. He tries to light a Kool through the incinerator, gives up, strikes a match. He doesn't have any place to sit. He leans against the incinerator concrete.

"That a Winston?" he asks after a time.

"Yeah," she says.

"You like Winston?"

"Mm-hmm."

She drops the cigarette on the ground, which is as much dirt as dried grass, and crushes it with her foot. She shakes the shoebox. Something solid is in there. Sounds like small pieces of something hard, not too heavy, a lot of them.

"My diamonds," she whispers.

"Huh?" Fields says. "You got diamonds in there?"

Mrs. Terrell thinks about whether she wants to muster the energy to tell her story, especially to this man who she's sure will miss the point anyway. But then the words just start coming out in a wave of raw emotion. She never looks at him; her eyes fix on one random empty square of the Cyclone fence separating her yard from the peeling clapboard duplex next door.

"That family I clean for, the Benjamins?" she says. "The lady of the house, she got a sister who lost her husband, and the sister got a little boy, and the little boy got real sick and had to stay home from the school for a week, but his mom, she work in an office and if she stay home to stay with him she'd get fired, so her sister sent me over there to stay with the little boy all that week. I didn't do nothin' that week 'cept stay with the little boy till his mom get home from work 'bout six. Just sat with him in a little speck of apartment not littler than your place. I knowed this little boy already 'cause he comes around with his mother to the house. Nice little boy. Nice, polite. Could already read. First day I showed him the racing pages, and I am not lyin', the boy picked four winners just by how he liked the name. You know, I called somebody I know and got two bucks down on two races, and the next day he got three more right. Made a few bucks for me. Now on my last day with him, we were for a walk around the block, to get air. There's a little island at the corner—you know you seen it—with that big old statue of some man from long time ago holding a pan supposed to be from a gold mined, and supposed to be real gold in there, so we went to sit on the rock for a spell, and when we were there, he saw these on the ground just lyin' there like they were waitin' for somebody to notice, and he reached down and he picked them all up in his hand, and he said, 'Mrs. Terrell, I want you to be happy. These are for you. You're rich now.' And he gave them to me in both my hands, and I said oh thank you and he hugged me and I kept them ever since. Two years about. Gonna be my treasure forever." She pauses a beat. "Passed on yesterday, that little boy. Gone to heaven."

She's crying now, real water down her cheeks.

Willie Fields doesn't know what to do.

Does he grab the box of diamonds and beat it out of there or break in to steal it sometime when she's at work? Tough decision, a lot of angles to consider. He doesn't know where she hides it, probably someplace good, so it'd be easier to pull the job now. Shit, he's got his wallet and keys in his pocket. He could just take the thing from her right this second and run. By the time she gets inside to her phone and calls the cops, he's blocks away. And come to think of it, what're cops going to do when they hear some old Negro lady crying about how some nigger stole her box of diamonds? Besides, how does she prove they're hers? If it ever comes to that, he can just say he found them, the way she did. All right, so that's the plan. There's nothing upstairs he can't live without if he never sees it all again; some clothes, that's all, the kind he won't want to wear anyhow when he's a millionaire. But where should he go? Any fucking place he wants. Maybe he'll go everywhere. He'll sell one diamond at a time in a different city each time, but first he'll take the biggest one to a jeweler and have it made into a fine pinkie ring. He's always liked those. Damn, all these months those diamonds were just in there, waiting to be snatched. She doesn't need them. They're not doing her any good. Hell, she owns this place, and diamonds aren't worth nothing if you don't sell them to buy other shit, so no harm's done.

"Can I see 'em?" he asks.

She hands him the box.

He can't believe she handed it over, just like that. He lifts the lid.

What? No, can't be.

Fuck. Is.

"Uh, Mrs. Terrell," he says, "these ain't diamonds. They broken glass, like from a pop bottle."

Mrs. Terrell squeezes her eyes for a second before turning her neck his direction to see, please, Jesus, that he was trying to be funny and cheer her up. Well, look at that. The man was sure enough serious. But the effect is the same anyway. She can't help laughing. Hearing the blues makes you less sad by pushing right on that spot. And stupidity—the real rare kind that's stupid through and through and doesn't know how stupid it is—gets you feeling better about yourself, too. The way seeing a cripple makes you grateful you can walk.

"God bless you, Willie Fields," she says. She pats his shoulder, takes the box and lid, and laughs once more but not in his face as she starts toward the house. "I pray He does."

Willie Fields is pretty sure something just happened, but right now he's too pissed thinking about the diamonds that weren't to think about what it was.

CHAPTER TWENTY-SEVEN

On his way home, Danny stops at Sunrise Market on the northeast corner of Seward and Willoughby, right across from where Walter Lantz
draws Woody Woodpecker. It's a little place that extends credit even to
deadbeats. The owner, Sam Steinberg, has a soft heart and memories of
when his own family had nothing during the Depression. Sometimes he
pretends to let customers pay off debts with a crummy old painting or
some avocados from the backyard tree. Sam's just two years older than
Danny, grew up in Minneapolis, was a state wrestling champion, has a
wife named Jackie and three young kids—Melinda, Jim, and Jeff. Until
the other day, Danny never thought he might ever want a piece of a life
like Sam's. Now? Well, maybe he does after all. Anyway, Sam is one of
those really good, solid, decent, honest, gracious men cops know too
few of, which is why, when Danny runs in for some Knudsen milk or
Olympia beer, he usually ends up talking about this and that with Sam
for half an hour, Sam keeping up the conversation while ringing up another customer's groceries with his right hand and bagging the stuff with
his left. And when Danny doesn't feel much like going home, he can be

there an hour or more, which is why he knows so much about Sam and Sam knows so much about him.

Danny's home is a pleasant Hollywood courtyard apartment. He hates being there, maybe because it doesn't feel like a real home. Especially lately. Two bedrooms and a bath around a small living room abutting a kitchenette with a little table against the wall covered in checkered vinyl that wipes clean with a wet sponge, just in case he ever eats there. The living room and a bedroom look out on a garden planted with annuals in the dirt area in the middle of the walkway that separates the two sides of the courtyard, three apartments on each. His is the back right, so he doesn't get people in front of his place unless they have the wrong address or are coming to see him, and that doesn't happen often. Total, eight other people are in the courtyard, three couples and two singles besides him. Of the eight, five are happy to have a cop around (when he's around), three get nervous when they see him, and six might be happier that he's a cop if the cop weren't Mexican. One thing Danny likes about this place is that garden. You can tell a lot about how fast an apartment's problems will get fixed by how well the garden's taken care of. The landlord really keeps it up. When the pansies die, he puts in some marigolds, maybe fuchsias or impatiens, and makes sure the ground cover is manicured nice. On this warm evening after a hot day with the cool night coming, Danny would like nothing better than to sit on the little concrete steps in front of his door drinking a beer. Well, not nothing better. And besides, cops shouldn't sit on their stoops drinking beer. Parker wouldn't like that.

Danny turns on the twenty-one-inch Emerson console in the living room, spreads the rabbit ears wide, and doesn't wait for the set to warm up before throwing his jacket on the couch and walking the five steps to the fridge, taking one Olympia from the six and leaving five. He sits at one of the two side-by-side table chairs, takes the .38 revolver from his shoulder holster, and puts it on the table. Makes a thump. Damn, the thing's heavy. It's like walking around all day with a boulder taped to your side, but you can get used to anything. If he ever forgets to bring it, 99 and then some percent of the days he'll be fine. Not often does he have to shoot. Hardly ever, actually. Still, the value of a gun is you know it's there, and they know it's there, and they know you can use it if you want to, and you know they know, which makes it less likely you have to.

The TV suddenly blares too loud. Danny forgot he turned it on. Now it's warmed up all the way and the announcer is saying be sure to stay tuned later for *Man Against Crime,* starring Frank Lovejoy, and there are scenes of the detective running after criminals in New York. Danny's never been there, but he's seen it enough on the screen to recognize it. Besides, he knows this show takes place in New York. Jack Webb himself told him that they were trying for a New York version of *Dragnet,* that the NYPD was jealous of what *Dragnet* was making the LAPD look like. But they couldn't pull it off. Whether that's true, who knows. *Dragnet*'s not on till Thursday. He'd always rather be out, but if he's not, Thursday's not a bad night to be home. At seven thirty he picks between *The Lone Ranger* and *Sergeant Preston of the Yukon* and then at nine it's *Dragnet.* He still gets a kick out of when somebody brings Friday a homicide and they keep up the running joke of his saying, "Give it to Galindo." It's been a while since Danny sold them a story. Maybe this one. No, never mind. They don't do rape either—and he's not sure how this is going to end. Danny hurries over and lowers the volume before switching the station two clicks to something called *Joe & Mabel,* one of those summer replacements they put on for thirteen weeks to give the regular shows a breather. Joe's a cabdriver in New York. Mabel's his girlfriend. She spends her days plotting how to marry Joe. Joe doesn't want to get married. It's supposed to be a laugh a minute.

Danny's back at the table. He uses the church key to pop two holes in the top of the Olympia and takes a long swig. He leans back and puts his feet on the table, the kind of thing his mother would've killed him for. All right, Danny, *Think. What do you have?* Suddenly, he can hardly hear the TV in the background; all he hears are his own thoughts.

Well, he has that Roark's not the guy. He has that the guy is a huge Negro and drives a late-'40s DeSoto, dark, maybe green, and no car like that was reported stolen, so it belongs to him. And he hits lovers' lanes for easy, young, gullible prey.

That's not much to go on.

Ever since Caryl Chessman, a bunch of moron crooks have pretended to be cops, but usually it's for robberies, and they're so stupid they're usually in jail before the night's out. Chessman had a fake cop light atop his car so he could get people to pull over in secluded areas. This guy goes to dark areas and flashes a fake badge. When the police catch him, the newspapers won't say anything about what he did; they'll just name him the "badge bandit," the way they named Chessman the "red-light bandit" because what he demanded of the women was what they ended up calling "an unnatural sex act." Compared to this guy, Chessman was an angel, and this guy's kidnappings are much more like kidnappings than Chessman's were; Chessman just moved them a few yards to get where he wanted them, and what he wanted from them was a lot less than this guy takes.

What if this guy's smart, like Chessman? Not smart after he's caught, like Chessman, who's clever about the law and in how he manipulates the system, but smart in how he breaks the law. As a criminal, Chessman was stupid, pulling robberies and finally knocking off a clothing store, where someone saw him and called the police, who chased him five miles up Vermont before catching this asshole who turned out to be the "red-light bandit" instead of some ordinary asshole crook. Even then, Caryl Chessman wasn't yet Mr. Big News. He was merely some creep grabbing stuff that didn't belong to him and trying to get blown on Mulholland by someone he'd just introduced himself to. If he'd stuck to that, he might still be out there.

That's something to think about. What if this guy's really smart in the way Chessman wasn't? He doesn't steal anything from his victims. He even tries to buy them something to eat, like it's a goddamned date, and somehow he keeps them from seeing his license plate. The only way to catch him, besides Parker or Mayor Poulson getting on the radio to tell kids not to neck at night in public—but no doubt they'd do it anyway—would be to pull over every Negro every night everywhere in the city. And that's not exactly practical. You'd need a lot more cops than are on the force; you'd need the army or National Guard, and whites wouldn't like it either because it would choke the streets. But even if you could do that, you'd still have to search every car from top to bottom for the badge and the flashlight, and that takes a blanket warrant. What judge would grant something like that? The city would have to be under martial law, like Germany after the war, when he was coming home. And by the way, there's no law against possessing a dime-store badge or a flashlight, and there won't be any fibers or fingerprints or hairs of the victims to cross-test on the badge and flashlight since they never touch his victims. *So what evidence are you taking him in on?*

No, it's obvious, the only way to catch this rapist is to catch him raping. Or run into him on the street with Margie at your side to point him out.

But wait, if Chessman is the guy's inspiration, where's he been the last six years that Chessman's been making a name for himself in the newspapers and on TV and in books? From the description, he's apparently in his thirties, so he didn't just come of age. And based on the car and his clothes, he's got a bit of money, so he's got a job—blue-collar, probably union, one of the trades. Too bad there's no way to compare union membership with DMV registrations. You might find something. Or you might not. Only one thing's for sure: you're not going to find anything by comparing bar memberships or state medical licenses against car registrations, which is actually something he could pull off with a little legwork, given how few Negro doctors and lawyers there are in L.A. It'd be a waste of time, though. No way some Negro who's somer-saulted over a fifty-foot wall surrounded by an alligator-filled moat for the right to practice law or medicine is prowling for poon after midnight.

Another waste of time is wondering why the guy does it. He does it because he can and because he wants to, nothing more. After all the rap-ists he's chased, Danny's no closer to figuring out why any man would think he's entitled to take what he wants from a woman who doesn't want to give it. Not having that inclination himself, he can hardly even imagine wanting anything more than getting lucky the old-fashioned way with a woman he's attracted to, though he suspects he's met more than one cop who, if he was honest, might be able to give him some insights into that. So far none of the guy's victims have been black, maybe because he fears being recognized around Negro parts of town—but more likely because Negro men would never fall for the "I'm a cop" routine. It's also possible he prefers non-Negro girls. If so, that's just tough luck, for him and everyone. Even as decent-looking as he's supposed to be, meeting and dating, let alone bedding, white women is a hard row to hoe. Just ask Todd Roark.

Did the guy come from another city? Danny doesn't think so. He checked, and no big city is looking for someone like this. Besides, there really aren't that many cities built for pulling off something like this—huge, mobile, anonymous, underpoliced. Which brings up a good point. This guy knows L.A. well, knows where the lovers' lanes are in the bet-ter but not best parts of town. That's not information you pick up fast here. So he's been here plenty long.

Danny finishes his beer and gets up, walks to the couch, reaches into his jacket's inside breast pocket for the map of L.A. he brought home, spreads it on the table over the gun, and lifts the pen from his shirt pocket. He takes a moment to orient himself geographically, then begins making X's with a circle around them everywhere the guy was reported to be, from where he ordered the couples out of their cars, to where he drove the young men, to where he took the young ladies, to where he let Margie and the marine out so close to headquarters (which is the one detail that so far has no plausible explanation in his imagination). Staring at the map, his eyes darting from one X to another, Danny tries to divine some pattern, something, anything—probably nothing the guy even knows he's doing; something subconscious.

Suddenly Danny realizes that this guy has assaulted a lot more ladies than are letting on. Of course. How could he have forgotten?

The insight sickens him. He knows it's true as surely as he knows the guy won't stop till he's caught.

God almighty, only a half, maybe only a third, of the victims are coming forward. A lot of women just refuse. Could be nine out of ten. They can't face it. And Danny can't blame them. People treat raped women differently afterward, as if they're not the same person—which is true, but not in the way the people treating them differently think. What's sad is that it's the courts that treat them worst of all. If the guy doesn't cop a plea and the thing goes to trial, she may as well be the defendant. Her life, her past, her everything is fair game on the assumption that women who've done it with someone will do it with anyone.

Danny goes to the fridge for another Olympia, reaches for a can, changes his mind, grabs his gun and jacket, leaves the TV on because now he doesn't see it the way he wasn't listening to it, walks out to his car, and heads south down La Brea. Maybe he'll run across a dark, DeSoto driven by a huge Negro who just happens to be showing his tin badge to a young couple.

CHAPTER TWENTY-EIGHT

MISSISSIPPI TEACHER TURNS LABORER TO RETAIN SELF-RESPECT

Robert F. Pierce, with 15 years experience as a teacher in Mississippi, now lives at 225 E. 28ᵗʰ St. because he refused to sign an affidavit saying that he had not contributed to the NAACP in Rankin County, Mississippi. He is a graduate of Jackson State College and Tougaloo College in Mississippi. He came here to work with his wife and three children. He has never voted, "but I paid my poll tax but they wouldn't let me vote."

L. A. SCHOOL BOARD BANS NEGRO TEACHERS

Most elementary school districts in Los Angeles County won't hire Negro teachers. School districts turn them away. There are 80 elementary school districts. The only ones willing to employ Negroes are Willowbrook, Compton, and Monrovia.

—Two articles that appeared in the *California Eagle* but not in any white newspaper—the *Los Angeles Times,* the *Herald-Express,* the *Examiner,* the *Mirror*—during the summer of 1956.

CHAPTER TWENTY-NINE

Willie Fields parks on Crenshaw and Vernon and walks past a storefront that says SPIRITUAL AND PSYCHIC READER. I PROMISE RESULTS WHEN OTHERS FAIL. NO FEE, DONATIONS ONLY. He doesn't know what that means even though he doesn't understand only one word.

Eddie's barbershop on Crenshaw is pissing distance from three or four other shops, all of them with barber poles turning out front. It's like barbershop row, and on Saturdays men crowd the block, so that's why he had to park so far. Willie Fields always goes to Eddie's, even if there's a wait, and there often is because Eddie's only has one chair. Other barbers charge the same fifty cents and give him the same haircut, but for some reason he likes Eddie's. A few years back he tried a white barber on the other side of La Brea. Like all white barbers, he was Italian—Joe Pinzone. And had no idea how to cut Fields's hair. He tried, though, then didn't charge Fields, knowing he'd botched it. For two weeks Fields looked like he had a relief map on his head because he didn't want to spring for a black barber to fix it.

When Fields walks into Eddie's shop, he sees someone in the chair

getting his hair cut and talking to Eddie, who doesn't look all that interested, so Fields sits down and picks up Thursday's *Eagle*. But now the
guy in the chair all of a sudden stops talking.

"Willie," he says. "Willie Fields."

Fields looks up, puzzled.

"It's Darryl, man."

No response.

"From work."

Still nothing. "The remodel on Graham. Local 300, brother."

Oh, yeah. Darryl. Fields didn't recognize him, what with the cape
around him and his being somewhere Fields didn't expect to recognize
anybody but Eddie.

"Yeah, yeah," Fields says. It's coming back to him now. "Yeah,
Darryl."

"How you doin'?"

"Good, yeah."

Same as work. There's no point trying to make small talk with this
guy who sings to himself instead of being friendly and all. Either Fields
isn't interested or—well, whatever. At least he's consistent.

"Be with you soon, Willie," Eddie says.

"Uh-huh."

Darryl picks up the story he was telling Eddie about the Battle of the
Bulge, how his unit ended up fighting alongside some white soldiers who
at first weren't too happy about it but then found the Lord when it became obvious that more white soldiers couldn't get to the Ardennes in
all that snow to bail out their asses. It was fierce fighting, and murder-
ous, the dead everywhere—bodies, body parts. "Stop me if I've told you
this before," he says, but Eddie wouldn't dare, even though he's heard all
this before, every word. Darryl keeps on talking about his heroics. Who
wouldn't?

Fields opens the newspaper. Flipping his way to the society page for

Dot's Dashes, he notices the words *New Orleans* and stops to glance over the story. It's about a Negro lady from L.A., traveling to New Orleans on the Southern Pacific, who was pulled out of the passenger car at the Texas-Louisiana state line and forced to ride the rest of the way in the baggage compartment.

Suddenly Fields feels a little homesick. He thinks about his wife Ruby and wonders if she's still his wife, whether they're actually divorced. He's not sure, hadn't thought about it before. She wrote to him a couple of times, but that was before he moved to this place and didn't let her know he'd moved. Maybe he'll let her know now. No, probably not a good idea. Besides, he might be moving soon anyway. Might have a different job, too. He'll wait and see.

On another page is an ad that says OIL MONEY SUPPORTS THE ARABIAN SLAVE TRADE. There's something about a ballot proposition, and Standard Oil, and how Negroes especially shouldn't support the Saudi Royal Kingdom because they still have black African slaves—half a million of them. "A NO vote against Proposition No. 4 is a vote AGAINST HUMAN SLAVERY," the ad says. So he's supposed to vote no, right? He reads a little more because it doesn't exactly say what they want from him. "Resolved, that the NAACP take cognizance of the United Nations report relating to slave trade in the Middle East and demand that the State Department discourage and eliminate the trafficking in human beings as it now exists in Saudi Arabia." Shit, what's that mean? How come they don't just come out and say vote so-and-so on so-and-so? Not that it makes a difference. He doesn't vote anyway.

Oh, no, *Dot's Dashes* isn't in this issue. It says Dorothea's in the hospital. The hospital? What for? It doesn't say. Fields hopes it's not serious. It would say if it's serious. Wouldn't it? Hey, look at that: Louis, Ella, and Art Tatum are going to be at the Hollywood Bowl. He'd like to see them, but only if he can sit up close. Nah, the Bowl isn't a good place for him. Besides, who'd he go with?

The guy from work is still in the chair, still yakking about the war. Fields closes the paper and notices on the table next to him a copy of last week's *Eagle,* too, which he hasn't gotten around to reading yet either. He picks it up, hoping Dot hasn't been gone two weeks. Good, there's her name in the small index box on the front page. Dorothea Foster, page 8.

Before he turns the page, a headline stops him. It's a story he kind of remembers overhearing the guys at work talking a little about because one of them knows one of the brothers involved. Fields wasn't paying too good attention when they were talking. Now he does.

DELLA HARRIS IN GETAWAY TRY says the headline.

"Lady, get back in that car! Get back in there and drive," the story begins.

"A man thrust a gun into the face of Mrs. Della Harris, wife of pharmacist Dr. Ellston Harris, 2717 S. Central Avenue, and forced her back into the car she had just parked.

"The man jumped into the front seat beside her, held his gun pointed at her, and snapped, 'Hurry up. Get started. Drive.'

"A second man pulled open the back door of the car, jumped in, and crouched on the floor. 'Drive,' came the command again. The gun to her head emphasized the words."

A gun, Fields thinks. *A fucking gun gets respect, that's for damn sure. Nobody doesn't bow to a gun.* The girl last night, off Ardmore, and also the week before—shit, pretty much all but one or two of his girls he's made love to recently would've gone easier and quieter with a gun to their head.

Now, for some reason, maybe magic, Fields tunes back in on Darryl's voice, still bragging on himself about the war. He's gotten to the part about how he and his buddies, white and black, walked through the snow after some awful fighting and collected souvenirs off dead Nazi soldiers. Darryl got something, too, he says; saw it sticking out of the boot of a dead man who'd had the top of his head blown off, the snow around him all red and gooey. He keeps it in a box at home—a pistol, nine millimeter. A Luger.

This is one of the few times, aside from when someone with tits walks by, that you could look at Willie Fields and know exactly what he's thinking.

CHAPTER THIRTY

As far as he can remember, and he's sure he'd remember, Danny Galindo has never before felt this way. Actually, he doesn't want to feel this way now, either, but there it is. It's not bad. It's fantastic. And also horrible. It hurts and feels spectacular at the same time—and against his better judgment, he doesn't want it to stop. He wants it to go on forever, damn it, and wonders whether this is what those sadomasochistic creeps he's popped over the years are aiming for when they do what they do.

The worst thing about it is how hard it is to do his job at a time when so much is on the line, with this really bad guy out there hurting people and Todd Roark suffering. True, this much is usually on the line; almost every someone who's hurt or worse has someone who suffers because of it. But now he himself is one of the someones, and he's got two great reasons for doing his job better than anyone else ever has. Too bad he can't seem to get one of those reasons off his mind long enough to do his job as well as a rookie patrolman would be doing it.

Half of what's going on is that he just can't believe this happened to him. After all this time. Under really peculiar circumstances.

He can understand victims falling in love with cops. But a cop falling in love with a victim? Thankfully, Margie's more of a witness than a victim, but just the same, she'll be taking the stand someday and telling about what happened to her that night when she sat beside this man who would've changed her life forever if he'd succeeded in doing what he intended to do and would have done if not for the quick thinking of another young man, that marine, whom Danny owes everything to and yet is jealous of. He knows what Margie told him about their relationship, that there was nothing between them. And he believes her. Even so, the marine got to kiss Margie once or twice. Or maybe he didn't. Doesn't matter. Really, it doesn't.

See how discombobulated he is? Pathetic. So that thought that's in his head right now—the one about going to pick up Margie again and driving around with her? Interviewing her as they go? Hoping she'll remember something useful? That's not a good idea. Not if he likes his job. And besides, it's total bullshit. Margie doesn't have anything else to add, and she won't until they catch this sucker. If it ever got back to Captain Lohrman, let alone Parker, that Danny was consorting with a material witness who's part of an ongoing investigation for any reason other than solving the crime, he'd be keelhauled—or whatever you want to call the cop equivalent. It would be horrible punishment. He'd lose his goddamn job, that's what would happen. Talk about not being able to live without something. The job means everything to him. It's his whole life. If he lost that, he'd have nothing. And nothing's worth risking having nothing. The faster he wraps this thing up, the faster he won't have to hide in the shadows with Margie, who, when you get down to it, may feel nothing for him. This may all be in his head. So there's no reason to risk anything.

Danny pulls up in front of Margie's rooming house anyway. He'd have called but he doesn't want the landlady to know he's coming. What difference that makes, he can't say. Luckily, the landlady's not there.

Another younger lady, probably one of the boarders, opens the door and runs upstairs for Margie. Margie is already carrying a light sweater when she comes downstairs. That means she figured out he wouldn't be coming if he didn't want to go somewhere, and her smile means she's happy to go.

They're already in the car at the curb when he asks if she's been to Pasadena yet. She says no. Would she like to see it? Very much. He explains that some men are in custody on a terrible rape case there, and he'd like her to observe them from a safe distance, to check whether one of them might be their guy.

"How many?" Margie asks.

"Five."

"Five? Oh, my. That's just terrible."

"Yes, it is."

"How old are they?"

"One's seventeen, two are eighteen, one's nineteen, one's twenty-two."

"So young."

"Yeah."

There's silence now, Danny waiting to see if she points out that these guys are *too* young—which they are—and hoping she doesn't.

"Okay," she says. "Let's go."

Well, he knows she's smart enough to have gotten the age thing, so her agreeing to go must mean she likes him. What else could it mean? Danny can't help smiling a little as he makes a U. Always the detective, testing, working. Of course, even though he's never been here before, he understands you can't really build a relationship the way you build a case. She'd feel as if he were always giving her the third degree, saying one thing and meaning another. The Cop 101 stuff. He'll have to learn how to be Mr. Galindo instead of Detective Galindo. For the time being, he'll just cruise on fumes and see where he ends up. Yeah, it's wrong to be doing this, but he thinks he can get away with it. If someone asks—Carpenter, most likely—he'll come up with just enough to keep it from being a whole lie. To tell the truth, doing something a little wrong feels kind of good. It's been a long time since he's felt so deep in the moment.

"How's the case going?" she asks.

"Roark's back in jail." He explains what happened, and that most cops are sure Roark's their man.

"That's so sad," she says.

"Yeah." But he can't leave it at that. "We'll find him."

They're pulling onto the Arroyo Seco Parkway, and he's about to tell her what it means in Spanish and how it got built in 1939, the oldest freeway in America, when she asks what crimes, exactly, these Pasadena accused rapists committed.

Danny really wanted to avoid the subject. It was the biggest reason he almost didn't do this, bigger maybe than losing his job, because of the distinct possibility that Margie would end up accidentally hearing what happened. For some reason, he didn't figure she'd actually ask. He thought the word *rape* would suffice. Now, if he tells her, she might assume that L.A. is as much of a cesspool as it really is, and she might want to move anywhere else.

"I don't think you want to know."

"Oh, I do," she says. "If I'm going to be in the same building as them and see them, I want to know what you think they did."

"It's not what I think. It's what the Pasadena police think, and what they already admitted to." Being defensive makes him crabby. There was no reason to split hairs. He softens his tone, asking, "You really want to hear?" in a way that says he's sorry.

"Yes. I really do," she says in a way that says she really does—and something about her clarity is incredibly attractive.

Eyes on the road, Danny pauses to breathe deep and compose himself. He drains his voice of emotion, keeping as much of a monotone as he can muster. Considering what he's describing, it's not easy.

A few nights before, a dazed seventeen-year-old girl and her twenty-two-year-old boyfriend wobbled into a Pasadena police station. The girl's face and other parts of her were bloody, and she could barely manage words into sentences to relate what had happened, but she had to be the one because the boyfriend's face was messed up too bad to talk, and besides he couldn't tell what he hadn't seen. The two of them, she said, had been parked in his car in front of Brookside Park. It was late, but they weren't necking, just talking. Five Negro males pulled them from the car and beat up her boyfriend—broke his jaw and knocked him out cold—before dragging her to a park table and taking turns with her. She was left lying there, naked except for what little remained of her torn clothes, too dazed even to cry, until her boyfriend came to and drove both of them to the station. Too bad neither of them could give a good description of the young men or the car. It was dark and happened too quickly. So if on the following night the five hadn't proved what Phi Beta Kappas they are, they might still be out there. They were driving in the same neighborhood and saw two fourteen-year-old girls walking. Their car screeched to a stop at the curb. Four of them jumped out, grabbed the girls, tried forcing them into the car. The girls screamed loud enough and fought back hard enough that the four gave up, got back in the car, and drove away. But not before one of the girls memorized the license plate.

Danny pauses here, to let it sink in for both of them that a license plate is probably the only thing keeping that fake cop on the street. He doesn't blame Margie. For whatever reason, nobody's been able to make it out.

"You'll like this," Danny says. He's looked over and seen that she hasn't liked any of this. "Cops found the car parked somewhere and impounded it, so when the owner called to report his car stolen, they told him it was at the impound yard for being parked illegally. The guy didn't wonder how come it was parked illegally. He just goes down there, and half a dozen cops point their guns at his head. Doesn't take two minutes for him to give up the other four."

The DA, Danny says, has already filed forty-four felony counts and announced he wants them executed, the juvies, too. Between them, they'd had a dozen previous arrests—robbery, firearms possession, loitering around school yards. And statutory rape: a twelve-year-old girl. All had done time somewhere. More than one stretch.

"You sure you still want to go there now?" Danny says. "You realize as well as I do we don't have to."

"We've come this far," she says.

They drive on for a while without a word. Danny exits the freeway. He seems to know where he's going. She doesn't realize that he's taking the long, scenic way around.

"Welcome to Pasadena," he says.

"It's pretty," she says. A mix of big homes on large, manicured lots, and some smaller ones, Craftsman, kept just so. Trees line every block. It's the kind of place you see in your middle-class, picket-fence dreams.

At the station, they play out the charade. Margie doesn't get closer than a hundred feet before announcing that none of them is the guy who took her for a ride.

"You want to hear something?" the Pasadena sergeant detective tells Danny. "The street where they tried to snatch those little girls? It was Lincoln. Lincoln Avenue." He coughs a cynical laugh. "Lincoln. The Great Emancipator. Look what he got us. Savages."

Danny glances at Margie. He's embarrassed, sure, but sooner or later she's going to have to know what he deals with every day—what the world is that he lives in. It's a world where a man's ugly words are the least-bad part. If that's too much for her, nothing he can do about it.

CHAPTER THIRTY-ONE

Here Willie Fields was feeling so pleased with himself. It had been a good night, and the guys on the job say they can always tell by his face Monday morning when Willie's feasted on some prime tail over the weekend. *So won't they be surprised when they see me that last night was a Wednesday? Me with a little Mexican girl. One little hot tamale I covered in hot sauce. De-lish.* That's what he's thinking as he crosses the framed-in doorway of the jobsite as the union dispatcher, a white man, is walking out. Fields tries to remember if he's ever seen the dispatcher on a job.

"Hey, Willie," the dispatcher says grimly and keeps walking. "Go get the news."

What news?

Darryl breaks it. When he sees Fields, he comes over from the group he was commiserating with to say Aloysius is dead. Aloysius Snypes, forty-six years old. Aloysius woke, same as always, dressed for work same as always, and was having his morning coffee at his neighbor's, Mr. Gardner, same as always when there was a knock on the door. Mrs. Dillon lives in the same building as Mr. Gardner, except he's on the first floor. She was outside and saw them and didn't know whom else to ask about being locked out of her apartment. They talked a little about tracking down the manager, who'd probably have a key, and she mentioned that she keeps her window open in the summer, seeing as how it looks out on the solid redbrick wall of the E.D. Troutman building next door. Nothing to see, in or out. That was when Aloysius said he could get through her window, no problem. He just needed to know which exactly was hers; he didn't want to go flying into someone else's apartment through an open window, he said, in case the people were there and didn't know to expect him. "They might think it was Superman." That's what he said. That's the kind of man Aloysius was. At any rate, he ran to his own third-floor apartment in the building on the other side of the Troutman building and crawled out and lifted himself onto his roof, then launched himself onto the Troutman roof and tiptoed along the edge till he was directly across from Mrs. Dillon's apartment. The window was four feet away but half a story down. Definitely do-or-die but a piece of cake—which was his last complete thought except *Oh, fuck!* He jumped, grabbed, missed, fell, and cracked his head on the walkway between the buildings. "You know what's really sad?" Darryl says. "He's got a boy, eighteen, just graduated high school, was just about to go off to Howard. Now he can't go. We're takin' up a collection for him. Mr. Charlie says the union'll match whatever we come up with. How 'bout it, brother?"

Fields had a hard time listening after Darryl said Mrs. Dillon was locked out. He kept wondering where she was just coming home from at seven in the morning, and wearing what? It didn't occur to him that she might've gone out in her robe to get her newspaper with the door slamming shut. And then the whole window thing sounded like Mrs. Terrell's husband, and for a second he thought they were the same guy, but only for a second or so, and because he was thinking so hard about it he's not entirely sure that he knows what's happening besides Aloysius not coming to work ever again. But yeah, sure, he'd be glad to chip in, he says, pulling a buck out of his pocket so the kid can go visit his friend Howard.

"Oh, brother, you can do better than that," Darryl says. "Think of that young man, just lost his father. Aloysius was so proud his boy was gonna be first one ever in his family to go to college."

"I got money," Fields says.

"Well, good then, brother, put it in."

"I got money to buy me a gun."

CHAPTER THIRTY-TWO

Carpenter's walking fast through the Police Administration Building, on his way to an interrogation room. He's in a better mood now. It had started off as one of those mornings when he heard that the big muck-a-mucks from the Methodist Church had voted to approve integration inside the church and condone it outside. He'd been born and raised Methodist, but for a moment he was mad enough to turn kike. Only for a moment.

What cheered him was the call from a buddy in Vegas, used to be LAPD before taking a better offer at the Dunes when it opened last year. As an old L.A. boy, he thought Carpenter would get a kick out of hearing that that Negro athlete Rafer Johnson, who plays a bunch of sports at UCLA and everyone says they like—well, turns out he won't be going to the Olympics in Australia after all. He's going to a Nevada prison. Forever. Anyway, that's what everyone in Vegas thought was happening for a couple of hours till they figured out that the nigger in custody is Raeford Johnson, not Rafer. Funny, huh?

"You called long distance to tell *that*?" Carpenter said.

No, the guy said. He called long distance to brag that Wild West justice, the best kind, is alive and well. And told him a story.

Carpenter liked the story so much that in the hour since he's passed it on enough times to cops who'll tell enough other cops who'll do the same that by noon every cop in the building will know what happened to Raeford, not Rafer, Johnson—and enough of them will be jealous enough of what the cops pulled off in Vegas that the odds of something like that coming true here, too, will go way up.

Maybe it'll start with Carpenter.

The interview room never looks different. Always that gunmetal table and chairs and scarred walls that are twelve and fifteen feet apart. Carpenter gets there before Roark. He's smoking a Lucky Strike when two uniforms lead Roark in, hands cuffed behind his back. Carpenter orders them to sit him down in a chair behind the desk and cuff his cuffs to the back of the chair. Ingenious. The only way Roark can stand is to lean forward, but then he'll have this heavy thing yanking his arms back. It's not strictly regulation except under the regulation pertaining to getting results.

Carpenter orders the uniforms to leave and go find Detective Galindo. They do so as he turns a chair around and sits backward, arms resting on top.

Roark's bad eye is either swollen shut or he keeps it shut to ease the pain.

"Want a cigarette?" Carpenter asks, holding up the half-smoked Lucky Strike.

Roark's yeah brings a smile from Carpenter. He knows Roark just realized he has to light it for him.

"Changed my mind," Roark says. "Giving it up."

"No, no, I insist," Carpenter says. He stands, pulls a smoke from his shirt pocket, walks slowly around the table, says, "Don't worry, I won't nigger-lip it," as he lights up with a Zippo. But it's Carpenter's own halfway-smoked Lucky he pushes toward Roark's mouth. Roark fights him as much as he can, all neck and shoulders. No match for Carpenter's two hands, one for the cigarette, one for the back of Roark's head. The cigarette is dangling from Roark's mouth when Carpenter goes back to his seat. Smiling.

Roark waits until Carpenter sits and has a good view of him before spitting the cigarette onto the floor. His left foot pulverizes it. Carpenter doesn't care. He's made his point.

"I want to tell you a story about a young man," he begins, deciding on the fly to leave out the Rafer Johnson mix-up. He says the young man is younger than Roark. He's twenty-two. An airman stationed at Nellis Air Force Base. And going to prison forever. Which he agreed to in exchange for avoiding the gasman.

The important part is that this whole thing, from crime to sentencing, happened in less than forty-eight hours. Just two days ago he raped a white girl. They caught him right away, he saw a judge right away, and right away he pleaded guilty, waived his rights to a trial and to an appeal, told friends and lawyers to beat it, and said let's get on with it already.

The door opens. Danny comes in and stops with his arm holding the door. Carpenter's back is to him. He can see that Roark looks worse and wonders if Carpenter heard him.

"Carpenter," he says.

Carpenter reaches back and waves him off without looking. He wants to finish grinding his point into Roark's forehead. He says he wants a full confession in ex—

Danny interrupts him. "Detective," he says louder. Then repeats it.

Carpenter spins around with poison eyes.

"Please," Danny says, motioning to the door.

One thousand one, one thousand two, one thousand three, one thousand four. Some of the red has gone from Carpenter's face when he finally stands and walks past Danny into the hallway, still wanting to tear

Danny a new one but needing to know what's so fucking important when he had the cocksucker on the ropes.

Danny just came from Newton division. Last night a young Mexican girl—an American who's brown, like Danny—came in complaining about being with her boyfriend in a car and then raped by a large Negro. The badge, the flashlight, the whole MO's the same. Carpenter says no, he'd have heard about that; the report would've been sent. But there's no report, Danny tells him. When the girl learned she'd have to tell everything officially and sign it with her real name, she took off. Still, it happened. Which means Roark's not the guy.

Carpenter says no, that's not what it means.

"He can't be in two places at once," Danny points out.

"Can't he?" Carpenter says. *Really, Galindo, how stupid can you be?*

He strides into the interview room, then stands at his full height with just the table between him and Roark, looking down at him, his voice a controlled rage.

"You thought we'd fall for that, you dumb asshole?" Carpenter says.

Danny takes a spot against the wall nearest Roark and struggles to keep a poker face, realizing what Carpenter's getting at—and knowing he's dead wrong.

"What're you talking about?" Roark says. He glances at Danny, who's fixed on Carpenter.

"Sending one of your little señoritas over to say a nigger raped her, and you expect me to fall for that?" Carpenter says.

"I don't expect you to fall for nothin'," Roark says. "But don't you insult my intelligence neither."

"Yeah? How's that?" Carpenter says.

"You think I'd think anybody'd fall for a dime-store badge? Come on, man, I was a cop. A cop, man. Same as you, I passed the test."

Carpenter's done. He looks at Roark with disgust and doesn't change a thing when he looks up at Danny before walking out.

Danny can't keep the poker face anymore, can't hold back his smile. That moment is something Todd can take back to his cell. It's nourishment for what might be long days ahead.

"Don't sign anything," Danny says. "No matter what."

CHAPTER THIRTY-THREE

Ol' H.H. is telling Willie Fields he might want to stop by the Rubaiyat Room to hear Ginger Smock and Her Swinging Strings, with Francis Carter on organ at the beautiful Hotel Watkins, Adams at Western. And he should know that the incomparable Amos Milburn is sitting in for a three-night stand this weekend at the 5-4 Ballroom. And he can hear Amos play what skyrocketed the man to stardom, a little thing called "Bad, Bad Whiskey" if he gets on over to Fifty-fourth and Broadway, in the heart of Watts.

But Fields isn't thinking about going anywhere except to Darryl's, on West Forty-sixth Place. He's on Forty-sixth now, slowing down, looking for 1838. Turns out he recognizes this street. Half a block away is a huge factory where he once put in some hours making roof tiles—work that just wasn't to his satisfaction. But Darryl's is a sweet little one-story Victorian with a porch out front. Fields parks and knocks on the door.

"It's for me," Darryl's voice shouts from inside, and a woman's says okay. Darryl opens the door a crack and slips through, fast closing it behind him so Fields can't see inside.

"Hey, brother, how you doin'?" he says.

Fields says, "I didn't know you was married."

"I'm not," Darryl says.

Fields makes that you-devil-you noise and grins big.

Darryl should leave it alone because what's the difference what this Willie Fields thinks? But he can't.

"My mother," he says.

Fields winces, like something hurt for a second. "Oh." What else can you say about that?

Darryl changes the subject by looking out on the street to check if anyone's around before reaching into the waistband of his trousers, under his untucked T-shirt, and pulling out the Luger.

"Here you go, brother," he says, handing it to Fields. "She's a beauty. I'll miss her."

Fields cradles the gun in his giant hands, turning it over to examine both sides, then puts it in his right hand and pivots right, pretending to take aim at the column.

"Whoa, brother, whoa," Darryl says, gently pushing his arm down. "Be cool. Nobody has to see this but us."

"Yeah, yeah," Fields says. He looks at the gun again and asks about the clip. It holds seven rounds but Darryl hasn't fired it in years so it might need some work, which is the reason he's letting this genuine Nazi war booty go for forty bucks. Fields hands him the wad in exchange for the gun. Darryl flips through the bills making sure they're all there. Fields positions the Luger in his waistband. Darryl doesn't ask what Fields wants the gun for; L.A.'s got a million reasons. Fields doesn't ask why Darryl's willing to sell it; money don't stink. Darryl doesn't volunteer that his mom needs new dentures.

CHAPTER THIRTY-FOUR

It didn't take Danny long to find out that Carpenter had told Roark only selected parts of that story about the Vegas airman sentenced to life two days after he supposedly raped a woman. He'd left out that the woman was wealthy. And married—to a prominent businessman who might or might not have mob connections and might or might not have pinned on Raeford Johnson something he'd done himself. Johnson volunteered the guilty plea at his arraignment on his own, no attorney present, after already signing away all his rights, including the right to appeal. Thirty days from an honorable discharge.

That must've been some beating. Or payoff. Or both.

Carpenter, at his desk, had overheard Danny learning all the details, repeating them back to whoever was telling him the info over the phone. Danny obviously wanted Carpenter to hear. It was a way of saying without saying that, at this point, Carpenter can't pretend anymore that this is about doing justice. And Danny can't pretend anymore he doesn't see that. Carpenter may really believe the real rapist is downstairs, back in his cell, and that Danny's a Mexican fool who should never have made detective. If so, that just proves how irrelevant Carpenter is now to the job of freeing an innocent man and capturing a guilty one. Any actual investigating will come from Danny—unless Carpenter manages to get him bumped off the case. Which isn't much of a possibility—unless Carpenter finds out about Margie and him. True, there's not much to tell yet, but what's there is more than Danny's career can stand if the wrong people want it to. Captain Lohrman, for example. Lohrman has known Carpenter ten years longer than he has Danny. A lot is riding on how clever Danny manages to be while doing his job. Maybe the way to cover himself is by hiding in plain sight.

He takes the "Badge Bandit" file to the cubbyhole they call the kitchen, where Carpenter's pouring himself coffee. "We should go see"—Danny opens the folder and pretends to read the name—"Margaret Bollinger," he says, convinced that Carpenter won't go anywhere with him.

"Who's that?" Carpenter asks.

"The first one. The lucky one." If Carpenter had ever seen her, Danny would have to acknowledge that she's also the pretty one.

"Why her?"

Danny can't give away too much without looking obvious. Whatever else he's become, Carpenter is still a detective; still has a dog's nose for bullshit.

"This Bollinger gal," Danny says, "might remember something different about the rapist than the others because she's not scarred by what happened."

Carpenter doesn't answer for a second.

Danny wonders whether Carpenter's letting him know he knows. Or could he really be considering the suggestion? No, out of the question. It better be.

"I was thinking about asking her to drive with us around Central for a few hours," Danny says. "It's possible the guy'll just pass by in his DeSoto and Bollinger will spot him."

"Yeah," Carpenter says, "you could get lucky."

Is he being sarcastic? Doesn't matter. Danny can't be bothered trying to guess how Carpenter meant that. He's in a hurry to get to Margie's before she comes home from her job. But bad news travels faster. Some of the cops he passes don't look quite as friendly as usual, even the uniforms. And when he walks by Olson, she calls out, "Hey, Galindo. You working security on the bullfight at the Pan Pacific?"

Some slick promoter nabbed a permit to hold a real *corrida de toros* in the auditorium off Beverly, figuring homesick Mexicans would buy all six thousand seats. Which they did.

"Not this time," Danny says. "It's a lady matador." True. "The kill takes too long."

CHAPTER THIRTY-FIVE

GANG FLOGS SOUTH CAROLINA TEACHER

CAMDEN, SC—Hooded vigilantes flogged a white high school band director last Friday morning for alleged pro-integration views.

Guy Hutchens, 52, bandleader at Camden High School, denied from his hospital bed that he ever advocated mixing the races.

Hutchens said he did not think the men were Ku Klux Klansmen.

Hutchens said his post-midnight ordeal occurred while he was returning from playing with the Charlotte North Carolina Symphony orchestra last Thursday night.

Hutchens said he stopped to change a flat tire and a car pulled up behind.

He said four or five men wearing masks hustled him into the back seat of their car.

They drove him about 50 miles then forced him out of the car, bound him to a tree and flogged him with switches and a board.

—An article that appeared in the *California Eagle* but not in any white newspaper— the *Los Angeles Times,* the *Herald-Express,* the *Examiner,* the *Mirror*—during the summer of 1956.

CHAPTER THIRTY-SIX

Willie Roscoe Fields is in a hurry to try out his new gun in the field. But he doesn't know how he's supposed to carry it. Right now it's lying on his bed. He's just staring at it. He wishes he had a holster and wonders if he should go to a toy store to buy a Hopalong Cassidy model.

This is his first gun, not counting the rifle the army gave him for about ten minutes. It's a beautiful thing. He pours a water glass half-full of some Hill and Hill scotch he bought on the way home—splurging four bucks for the good stuff at Goldilocks Liquors—with the Luger in his waistband, which is how he knows that he needs to find a better place for it. For one thing, it's uncomfortable. For another, he doesn't like the barrel pointing down his pants that way, right at his dick. The thought of something happening to it by accident gives him the shivers. Shit, you might as well put a second bullet through his brain right at that moment. Living without his dick isn't an option.

Fields drains the glass in a few gulps and refills from the bottle. He glances out the window into the backyard. No Mrs. Terrell. The incinerator isn't even going. But he draws the blind anyway. The room is darker. He flicks on the table lamp. Now he picks up the gun in both hands, feeling its perfect weight. He transfers it to his right hand, arm down at his side, the Luger comfortable, as if he'd been born with the appendage. He turns to the dresser mirror. Too bad. The reflection is cut off at his waist. He can't see the gun, even if he stands on his toes, until he leans over the dresser and gets his head close to the mirror. Yep, there it is, in his hand. Doesn't do any good, though, since he can't exactly walk around carrying the thing. Sad.

He leans back and with his left hand picks up his glass of booze, watching himself as he finishes it, very Humphrey Bogart, the gun held diagonally across his chest. It fits there. Or it would if he had something to hold it in place. Wait, maybe he does.

From a drawer he takes two belts and connects them, putting the prong of one through the last hole of the other. He fits the length over one shoulder and beneath the other armpit before tightening and fastening the two free ends at his side, fashioning a poor man's bandolier. He stands in front of the mirror enjoying himself—Pancho Willie— and slips the gun between the belt and his shirt. It slides down. He tries again, this time arching his back to keep the strap taut. That works, but to what end? No, without a holster, the only way to transport this thing is in a pocket. He drops it into the right pocket of his trousers. Oops, too close to his dick again; and it looks like he's got a really big bone daddy. Bigger than usual. Which is saying something.

Fields opens his closet and takes out his nicest sport coat, the shiny one, dark brown with yellow stitching. He slips it on and tries out the gun in the inside breast pocket. Pretty good fit, as long as he doesn't button it. That's all right. He doesn't need to. All he needs is that brown-and-yellow silk tie with the palm trees that he stole from the Salvation Army secondhand store. He ties it nice, checks himself in the mirror, likes what he sees, then pulls the gun out and holds it to his head, just above the right ear.

"Shut up and be quiet," he says. And repeats that different ways, more menace and less, each of the five times he rehearses, careful to avoid touching the trigger.

CHAPTER THIRTY-SEVEN

Danny parks on Ingraham across the street from Margie's, his car pointing in the direction from which she'll be walking from the bus. That
way he can jump out the moment she appears. It takes half an hour till
her head bobs above the parked cars. Jesus, is he glad to see her. And
she him. Thank goodness. And he likes that she doesn't say she needs to
run up to her room to powder her nose or put on a new face or change her
clothes. Most girls would.

"All right, Detective, where to tonight?" she asks.

Danny is dying to tell her to call him Danny. But that would be a
terrible idea. What if they're at the station or somewhere with other cops
and she lets that slip? It's okay for him to call her Margie now because
he can trust himself to remember to call her Miss Bollinger. On the
other hand, till this thing is over—and that could be months from now,
even if they catch the guy tonight—hearing the word *Danny* out of her
mouth is as close as he's going to get to a kiss.

"Call me Danny," he says.

"Danny," she says, smiling. "I knew you were a Daniel. But I didn't know if you were a Dan or a Danny."

Danny's torn between wanting her to see the good side of L.A. for a change, and needing her to drive around a bit with him through the much wilder streets in a part of town that's not like anything else she's ever seen, considering where she's from. Of course, you could say the same about the good side. There's no place like L.A.

"We can do both, can't we?" Margie asks.

No reason why not, and that's excellent news for Danny.

"You okay to get home late?" he asks.

Of course.

"What about work tomorrow?"

It'll be fine.

Danny checks his watch. Still early. Too early, probably, for the guy to be out and about yet. The rapes were all long after midnight, and some of the girls remember the booze on his breath, Margie because she sat so close to him in the car. Even if he drinks at home, though Danny suspects he enjoys Central's nightlife and wishes he, too, were parked legitimately with a girl on a lovers' lane, it doesn't seem likely that he'd drink more than four hours straight before attacking; he'd be too loaded to do it. Which means they still have a few hours free.

Danny drives north up Vermont, all the way into Griffith Park, telling her the story of the crazy old coot named Griffith who donated the property to the city as penance after doing time for shooting his wife. Danny heads west on Sunset as the sun sets straight in front of them, cuts up to Hollywood for a while at the good part—not his neighborhood—where she can see Grauman's Chinese and the restaurant shaped like a big brown derby, then back down Sunset into Beverly Hills. Crossing Doheny, he tells her about the crazy old coot who pretty much jabbed a tree branch into the ground and struck oil before getting caught up in a bribing scandal that ruined President Harding's reputation. He drives up

Bellagio and tells her about the crazy old coot who didn't have two nickels when someone discovered oil on his farm about fifty miles east and south, and with his hundred grand a week from the oil lease—when that was serious money fifty years before—Alphonzo Bell decided to buy a couple of thousand acres to subdivide into what he called Bel Air. They wind their way up the hill to Mulholland Drive, overlooking the Valley, and Danny explains how it was named for the man who more than anyone else was responsible for L.A.'s being what it is by making sure there was wet stuff, not sand, when people turned on their taps, bringing water hundreds of miles from where God intended to where He didn't. William Mulholland made a lot of men sensationally rich but not himself, and he died broken after the last dam he built, just north of the city, busted one March morning, 13 billion gallons of water becoming a forty-mile torrent of mud, garbage, trees, animals, cars, houses, and bodies—five hundred of them, some of which were found floating weeks later far out in the Pacific.

"You know a lot about Los Angeles history," Margie says.

"Well," he says, "it's all written in asphalt. Most cities, streets are named for trees and presidents and numbers. In L.A., they're for men who did something to get their names on a sign," *which means the whole city is either a con or a crime scene.* "In just a few years, maybe thirty, it went from a few thousand people to millions. I only know a few names. The big ones."

Actually, Danny knows much more than that. He knows about the birth of the city and the armed sentinels who patrolled in the late eighteenth century; knows about the Spanish missions and the decline of the Indian population when they were moved out of the missions to work commercially; knows that L.A. was reputed to be the "most evil city in California" and why those who thought they could prosper in that environment came here; knows about the armed marauders who terrorized the area; knows about the Chinese Massacre of 1871 and vigilante uprisings and impromptu firing squads, and about the rise of ethnic gangs and the Black Hand Society; knows that within a matter of decades L.A. became the world's largest city in area—and has remained, beneath the sunshine and smog, just as outside the law as it used to be.

"You like it here?" Margie asks.

"I do," he says. *God help me.* "This place has everything, and I mean everything. And everyone. What we're seeing isn't even a tenth."

They're still on Mulholland Drive. Danny pulls over east of Benedict and, pointing to the lights, says this is the most famous lovers' lane in Los Angeles, probably the world. Margie says she can see why.

And you know what? So can Danny. Before, he only recognized the fact. Now, he gets why it's a fact.

He also gets that if he doesn't drive away this very second, they might be there all night.

He pulls a U, heads south on Benedict, and turns east on Wilshire, remembering to tell her about the crazy old coot real estate developer who was seriously a socialist, which is a strange political belief for a rich capitalist.

Margie hasn't said anything, but she's got to be hungry. Danny just realized that they haven't eaten. So where to stop? It's tempting to sit down at a real restaurant with food and drinks—tempting but stupid. Also foolish. Staring at her across a tablecloth through candlelight without wanting more would be a weight he might not be able to lift, especially after a glass of wine.

"Let's get some grub," he says. "You like hot dogs?"

Who doesn't? She laughs when he pulls up to Beverly and La Cienega beside the Tail o' the Pup, a hot dog stand built to look like a hot dog in a bun with mustard on it. At eight thirty on a balmy August night, with teenagers everywhere in these last weeks of summer, their passing cars with the windows down and radio up playing Elvis and Little Richard and the Cadillacs and the Platters and Vic Damone and the Coasters,

Danny and Margie have to share one of the outdoor tables with another couple, meaning there isn't much they can really talk about. The other couple is gossiping about people they know. They don't seem to mind anyone else listening.

Danny asks if Margie likes her hot dog. She says it's delicious. He doesn't know how it can be. She put only a drip of catsup on it instead of mustard and relish and sauerkraut.

They both pretend to look elsewhere so that they're not looking at each other. He's stuck staring east, over her shoulder, at the Owl Rexall drugstore. He'd planned to tell her about Carpenter and Roark and the airman, and then he was going to tell someone for the first time about flying during the war, when he was a bombardier with the 445th, and a damned good one, one of the best. He might even have told her about his last mission, how their B-25 was hit on the way to take out a bridge in the Brenner Pass. Over northern Italy, German artillery sent up a barrage of shells, hitting several airplanes in the squadron, downing three. On Danny's airplane, high-octane fuel was pouring out of a gaping hole in the left wing, and that engine was in flames. One guy, Miller, bailed immediately. The rest of the crew stayed, and Danny kept dropping ordnance by hand. Only when they clearly had no alternative did everyone else—from pilot to turret gunner—bail and deploy their parachutes. So not till after the war, not till after he'd survived the Stalag (for a second time; no escape this time), not till after the incident reports were in and described how Lieutenant Daniel Galindo had shown incredible bravery, did he learn that some son of a bitch bastard piece of shit motherfucking asshole was trying to make himself look better by claiming that it had been "the Mexican-American bombardier" who'd jumped right after the plane was hit. No surprise, the liar was Miller, the coward who'd jumped on impact. Which, as a matter of fact, is what worries Danny about Carpenter. Guys like Carpenter who don't know what they're made of under fire always feel a little threatened by guys like

Danny who do, especially if the guys like Danny have last names that end in vowels. The only way Carpenter can make himself feel better is by tearing someone else down. He won't hesitate to do that with Danny.

But Danny doesn't say any of that. Instead he turns around to see what Margie is looking at over his shoulder with such obvious pleasure. It's that little amusement park next to a pony ride, Beverly Park, which everyone calls Kiddieland. The ponies are open only on weekends. But you can still smell them across the dirt ring.

"Do you want to go in?" he asks her.

"We have time?" she says.

Danny checks his watch. "Yeah. Come on."

He puts out a hand to help her up and leads her around the corner onto Beverly. It's free to walk in, but you have to buy tickets at the booth to ride the carousel, Ferris wheel, dodge cars, roller coaster, miniature train, or little boats that go around the aboveground plastic pond. A calliope plays the same thirty-two bars over and over.

Margie's face shines. Which makes Danny like the place more than he usually does, because he usually doesn't. This must be how parents get when their child accomplishes something for the first time that they've done a million times; in fact, it's what half a dozen parents at Kiddieland look like right now. Danny wishes he and Margie had all night to spend here, which reminds him that if it weren't for this bad hombre, he'd never have met Margie. It's an odd thing, kind of like the way manure makes gardens grow. He thinks about buying a couple of tickets from the teenage boy in the booth over there behind the old NCR register. Maybe they'll go on the dodge cars. Never mind. That might seem too much like a real date.

Too bad, though, for the teenager that Danny spotted him.

"Excuse me a second," he says, leaving Margie by the train. He walks to the booth and waits while a man buys some tickets. Now it's Danny's turn.

"How many, mister?" the kid says. He's wearing a striped, short-sleeve shirt with the sleeves cuffed and his hair cut in a flattop that in the lights shines from pomade.

"Two," Danny says, handing him a dollar.

The teenager gives him two tickets and two quarters that were lying on the black lip of the register. "Here you are. Thank you."

Now Danny leans over the counter and whispers, "What's your name?" in a cop's voice.

The kid gulps and says, "Buster."

"Buster?" Danny says. "No one's named Buster. Buster's the name of one of the ponies over there, isn't it?"

"Yes, sir."

"So what's your real name?"

"Ron."

"Listen, Ron," Danny says, "I know you're skimming cash, not ringing up sales. Some of it goes in your pocket. Maybe a lot. What you should know is that Mr. Bradley who owns this place—Dave's a friend of mine. And I always take care of my friends." Danny steps to the side and opens his jacket just enough to show Ron the gun. "Now, would you like an opportunity to make good?"

Yes, Ron very much would, and he promises to empty every last penny from his pocket into the register, even what he got paid, and Danny promises to surprise him with visits that Ron won't see coming till Danny's right in his face.

Danny hates to tell Margie they're leaving. Danny hates to leave. They'll come back when this is all done.

CHAPTER THIRTY-EIGHT

"It's pawtee time," Willie Fields says. He feels good dressed in his best coat and tie, gun comfortable in his inside pocket in case he needs it, studying the marquee of the Brass Rail, that little club Darryl told him about on Broadway and Vernon. Normally Fields doesn't like to hop so far from Central, but Darryl said it was a burlesque joint, and to Fields, *burlesque* is another word for *naked*. And yeah, that's what it says outside in not so many words; it says that something's shaking at the Brass Rail seven nights a week. It sure do look that way, what with smiling photos of the Joy Jumpers Orkestra, Marvin "Golden Voice" Fullove, Rockin' the Blues, and "Smiling" Smoky Lynn providing the backing for a bevy of beauties too beautiful to show, obviously, from the neck down. Their faces are okay-looking, but that's not what he's come to see.

Fields pays the buck cover charge for the second of three floor shows set to start in just a few minutes, the man in the white shirt and black bow tie tells him. He can have a table down front if he wants, but Fields doesn't want to sit there alone, all eyes his direction when the show begins. He sits at the bar in the back of the room and orders a double bourbon, please, from bartender Olin Gore, who tells Fields that he co-owns the place, so if he has any complaints, he knows where to direct them. Fields takes it that the guy's bragging, so as long as they're bragging, he has a good mind to say something about his gun and how he's fucked five hundred women, give or take.

Fields lays a buck on the bar and swivels toward the stage. Half a dozen couples and three foursomes are at tables on the floor. Two other singles are farther down the bar, one against the wall. Fields doesn't feel bad, though, not being part of a crowd. He knows he's got a date later that night, knows that he'll be making love with someone new a little after midnight. Just him and her in his car. And a gun to her head keeping her quiet so he can do his magic. He taps his chest lightly. Good, still there.

The guy who collected his money at the door is suddenly onstage. He says his name is Leroy Daniels and introduces the Joy Jumpers Orkestra before calling out the first of the night's exotic dancing beauties, the one and only Valda Gorez. She's not naked and doesn't get naked. Neither does Cathy "YoYo" Cooper, despite her promising name, Anna "Specialist" Louise, or Lawanda, goddess of fire. What a fucking beat.

Fields has had four of those double bourbons at a buck each and is in no mood to leave Olin Gore a tip. Besides, the fellow owns the place. That would be like tipping Eddie the barber.

What he's in the mood for is one thing only. But walking down Broadway to his DeSoto, the street alive with cars and people, he's not walking fast. He's walking tall. He's strolling. He's styling. He's looking at people's faces in the streetlight, no fear. They don't see him. He's their god, he's their master, he can kill any of them if he wants to. He's feeling the power of that gun on him, and in a weird way it reminds him of sex. True, everything does. This is different. This is what it would be like if he had two dicks, which he's thought about before. For a second he's torn between wanting to find a place where he can shoot something and wanting to find that night's girlfriend and seeing how she reacts to him and his gun—Mr. Two Dicks. He decides on love first, and then if he still wants to, he'll find somewhere to shoot something.

Who the hell would ever choose shooting over fucking?

CHAPTER THIRTY-NINE

It's a long drive south and east to Central Avenue. On the way Danny and Margie pass near some of the lovers' lanes where girls reported being raped by this guy. Danny mentions when they're close but doesn't drive by. He wants to tell her that if he'd been in a car with her instead of the marine, the guy would be off the street right now. But of course, how could Danny have met her if not for the guy? He can't stop thinking that.

To change the subject in his head again, he explains how hard it is to catch serial rapists. Most of them work a particular area, as if it's their territory—familiar and safer. They know all the tricks, shortcuts, dark places. So you can send plainclothes cops to patrol discreetly, pretending they're just regular people. What would work best and fastest is a lady cop dressed a certain way, but there aren't any lady cops Parker trusts to survive walking down the street advertising themselves as rape bait. Still, if you watch that area long enough with some plainclothesmen, you'll catch him. He'll make a mistake, and that'll be that.

This guy, though, he works wherever he can find lovers parked, which in L.A. might be anywhere.

Danny says it would be a lot easier if Carpenter and the other cops and the DA weren't so sure they'd already caught their man. He could assemble a task force and dispatch a dozen unmarked cars every night. But being alone on this—well, until someone brings in the guy's wallet or license plate, catching him will be pretty much a pure dumb accident of fate; Danny will have to drive in circles around places where someone who does what the guy does in the way that he does it might spend his nights. Danny says that unless he thinks of something clever, he just has to hope that that's what happens.

It occurs to Danny that Margie might think he's asking her to spend every night cruising with him in search of a dark DeSoto and its driver. He's about to clarify that he's not doing that when he changes his mind, because maybe he is.

CHAPTER FORTY

From Broadway, Willie Fields zags onto Figueroa and cruises north, past the Coliseum and the museums, past the college and the Shrine Auditorium, and then under that new Santa Monica Freeway thing, which he refuses to drive on, and almost just like that the property values rise—and it's a little more dangerous being Negro after dark. He hangs a left on Venice and turns west, knowing that if he stays straight to the end another dozen miles he'll see the Pacific Ocean, which he's never seen in his ten years here. Tomorrow, maybe. In a while he turns up Western and a mile later veers onto Eleventh Street. He knows where he's going. The corner of Manhattan Place has no streetlamps, two small houses, a redbrick apartment building with New York fire escapes, and a sweet little vacant lot facing north toward the hills where you can see lights twinkling, should you need to pretend you're parking for the view. Even if they wanted to, the people in the apartments and houses can't see what happens in those cars parked on the dirt, which explains why the people in those cars park there.

Fields stops on Eleventh just short of Manhattan, in front of a house instead of the apartment, and kills his lights and engine. A Dodge is parked at the far end of the lot. It's the only car there, and swear to God, unless he's seeing things, that car is rocking. Yes, sir. Someone's doing the dirty inside. He sure hopes they're still doing it when he gets there.

From the glove box he takes the flashlight and the badge, then wonders how to pull this off. With the gun now, he's got three things but only two hands. He can't hold both the flashlight and the gun in the same hand; they're too big. And he can't hold the flashlight and badge in the same hand, because then he can't shine the flashlight on the badge to let them see he's a cop. How about the badge and gun in the same hand? That would mean he'll be shining the light on the gun, too. Fuck it. He's got a gun, he doesn't need a flashlight or badge. But then if he doesn't bring a badge, what right does he have to arrest them?

Fields tiptoes across the dirt. It's not necessary, though, as he realizes when he gets twenty yards away. He can't see through the fogged windows, but the girl inside is definitely enjoying herself, moaning loud enough to drown out whatever Johnny Magnus is saying on the radio. There ain't a better sound in the world—or quicker way to get him hard. He slides out the gun. "You love me?" she manages to pant before answering her own question three times in the affirmative. And then talking to God. Fields can't take it anymore.

He raps the gun barrel on the driver's window and says just loudly enough so no one else but them can hear, "Vice squad." The girl shrieks as Fields yanks on the door. It wasn't locked and opens, the dome light coming up like a spotlight on a much better show than the one he just came from. A pretty little thing, can't be more than seventeen, in a plaid skirt with no undies and saddle shoes, her white blouse open to the waist and bra hiked under her neck, straddles a guy about twenty, his blue jeans down to his knees. The girl jumps off him. She looks terrified and the guy probably does, too, but Fields sees only the girl, everything

about her—every last delicious, young thing about her—until he notices
that the guy's got a rubber on his now limp dick.

Elvis is singing not to be cruel.

"I don't have to be telling you two that you committing a morals violation," Fields says, showing the badge for only a second and then the
gun again. "Get out, young man."

John Calgrove turns off the radio and pulls up his jeans. Nancy, who
will never give her name or make out in a car again, is trembling as she
straightens her brassiere and buttons her blouse. She doesn't know what
to do about the undies on the car floor. Her knees are slammed together.

"Come on, get out," Fields says, using the gun as a pointer. He's eager to have a go at his catch before she cools down. Calgrove gets out.
Fields leans toward Nancy. "And you stay right there," he says. "I'll be
back for you soon as I take your man to jail." He's so on for this girl
that even her crying can't erase what's in his mind, and for a second he
wonders why not just get right to it—shoot this sucker dead right now
and pick up where he left off with her riding him. Or he could just
pistol-whip him the way he sees it done on TV; the guy who gets
whacked wakes up a while later with a headache but nothing else wrong.

"Let's go," he tells Calgrove, pushing the gun into his back, urging
him toward the street.

"Where to?" Calgrove asks.

"My car's there," Fields says.

There's not enough light for Calgrove to make out what it is. He
doesn't care anyway. He's young but not green. He's from New York.
He says, "Hey, listen, Officer, isn't there a way for you to forget this?"

"I can't forget what I saw." Fields says. Which is true. "What do you
mean?"

"Maybe, I don't know, five bucks to make this go away."

Fields always thinks that his marks believe he's a cop, that they buy
his angle. That's how swift he is. So he misses the pleasure of realizing

that this junior Mr. Charlie actually does think he's a plainclothes vice officer, otherwise he wouldn't have tried to bribe him. Only a cop—a crooked cop, of course, but that's a given—would take the money and look the other way with a pretend warning. The real bad guy's going to help himself to your cash anyway, then do what he wants to do.

"Keep going," Fields says.

"I might be able to come up with ten," Calgrove adds, misunderstanding.

They reach the street now and begin crossing to the other side where the car's parked. Calgrove sees it's a DeSoto but that's all he can see. Fields stops behind it, blocking the license plate, even if he's not trying, and tells Calgrove to let himself in on the passenger side. He watches to see Calgrove doing that before climbing into the driver's seat and closing the door. Only for a second did the dome light shine on Fields's face—enough to show Calgrove that something worse than he thought is coming.

To aim the gun at his passenger, Fields has to hold it in his left hand, so he does all the shifting and steering with just his right. Driving that power buggy at work has helped sharpen his skills.

"Where we going?" Calgrove asks.

Fields pulls onto Ninth Street, then over to the curb in front of a duplex. "Where's that ten bucks?"

"Sure, sure." Calgrove says. He fishes out two fives from his pocket—all the money he has—and hands them over. "Thank you. I'm here visiting from out of town, and she's my friend's who I'm staying with's sister, and she's only sixteen, and she—"

The outcome's already fixed anyway, but that's still not the sort of thing to be telling Willie Roscoe Fields. A sixteen-year-old who already knows how to fuck? Maybe New Yorkers aren't as street-smart as they pretend, or maybe John J. Calgrove just wanted to believe what he wanted to believe because believing what he could see was just too awful.

"Get out," Fields says.

"What?"

Fields shows the gun and Calgrove can't argue with that kind of logic.

CHAPTER FORTY-ONE

Central Avenue is crowded, cars in the street and people on the sidewalk. Danny pulls over in front of a liquor store and resists telling Margie to keep her door locked. Instead he says he'll be right back. He manages his way across the paths of everyone walking and goes inside the store. Today's Thursday. So the *Eagle* is new today. Danny picks it off the news rack below the register and buys a copy for a dime. MAN CUT IN HALF BY P.E. TRAIN is the banner headline above the front-page story about a thirty-year-old on Twenty-ninth Street who'd had a bottle of Thunderbird too many and fell under the passing Pacific Electric train while trying to impress his friends with an acrobatic trick.

Walking back to the car, Danny wonders if Margie has ever been in the minority around so many Negroes, but decides she probably didn't even notice. She's like that, completely without prejudice, exactly the opposite of everyone else in his world. Sure enough, when he gets in the car, her smile is easy and quiet. It's a haven, and he can imagine coming home to it every night to treat the day's sickness.

"Get what you need?" she asks.

"We'll see," he says.

He flips the black plastic switch that turns on the dome light and opens the *Eagle* to the entertainment pages, looking for where their guy might get his kicks. That could be anywhere. Pete Jolly and Amand Ross are at the Tiffany Club. Les Brown's at Zardi's. Players he's never heard of are at Club Adshaw and Club Oasis, and no one's at Dynamite Jackson's; it's just a cocktail lounge. There are too many possibilities. Danny hates guessing. He appreciates a more scientific approach. But when all that you know about someone is the worst thing about him, guessing what kind of social entertainments he likes pays off less often than Irish Sweepstakes tickets.

Most of the clubs are along Central or Crenshaw, with a few over on Western. In between are burger stands and lounges and restaurants. He'll just drive the most crowded parts of all three streets, and maybe he can show Carpenter he really did get lucky.

Danny tells Margie the plan and again asks if she's up to it. She is. "All right," he says, "just concentrate and see if you see him walking," which she does. "I'll watch for dark DeSotos," which he does but also watches for guys who might look enough like the sketches.

That guy? No. That guy? No. That car? No. And so it goes.

"You know what?" Margie says. "If we ever go on a real date, it'll be boring."

CHAPTER FORTY-TWO

Willie Roscoe Fields has circled back and pulled alongside the Dodge, pleased to find Nancy still sitting inside, still trembling, still terrified.

She asks where John is.

"Where he belongs," says Fields, appreciating how he's not lying but still being a cop. "Your turn," though he's thinking, *My turn*. "Get in, young lady." He shows the gun. She complies. She would have anyway.

Fields turns the other way up Eleventh so that he won't cross paths with Calgrove.

"You're a policeman?" she asks.

"Deputy sheriff."

She doesn't know the difference and couldn't think about what it means even if she did. All she knows is that she's going to be in trouble. And she's petrified. When her parents find out, she might have to kill herself. If her father doesn't kill her first. Oh, Jesus. *Damn, damn, damn*. Why did she do this? Her older brother was home from college back East for the summer and asked his friend John to visit. John grew up in New York and had been hitchhiking all over the country anyway, having lots of adventures. He was twenty. And cute. He winked at her over the dinner table the first night and got up in the middle of the night a couple of nights and went to the bathroom just to see if maybe her bedroom door was open, or maybe she might be coming out of the bathroom. And one night she actually was, wearing the nightie she'd worn every night since the wink. He smiled at her. He had a way of smiling at her. It made her feel very different in a very good way—all grown-up. Like him. And then her brother suddenly had to work the next night, filling in for someone, and when John volunteered to take her to the movies, her parents didn't think anything strange about that, since he was their son's friend from college. So she pretended to say yes reluctantly, and then she and John settled on saying they were going to see something at the Four Star on Wilshire called *The Killing,* about a racetrack robbery, because he'd already seen it and could tell her about it on the way back in case anyone asked at home. John wasn't one of those squares from school, or even like that older kid Dustin Hoffman from the year before who thought she was something. John just kind of made her want to touch herself, and he was going back to New York, so if something ended up happening between them, well, the guy would be gone and no one at school would ever hear about it—as long as she didn't get pregnant. And of course, he promised that he'd wear a rubber to keep that from happening. And so she said yes, and it was feeling even better than she'd hoped, which is saying something, until—boom. Like a house falling on her. And now here she is, on her way to being in really terrible trouble.

Too bad she went to L.A. High. If she'd gone to Jefferson or Crenshaw or another school south or east of there, where whites are used to seeing fewer white faces, she'd have learned if only by osmosis that Negroes aren't plainclothes vice cops or any other kind of cop who do this, and instead of waiting for the "huge Negro" to come back, she'd have run like hell and found help when he took off with her date on the other side of a gun.

The way he keeps glancing over at her makes her uncomfortable. The third time he does it she notices something and realizes this is not what he says it is, which means she figured it out faster than John Calgrove. It takes her only a second to get over that it can't be happening.

She's right not to let on that she knows. She'll wait till they stop next and jump out and run screaming for help. But they're not stopping. All the lights on Olympic are green, one after another, and at this hour there isn't much traffic. She prays for a cop car and slowly reaches for the door handle.

Willie Fields knows the longer he's with this blond girl in the car, the better chance there is of someone seeing. Doesn't matter who. Could be anyone. Anyone white would call the cops. Maybe black, too. Since they got in the car, he hasn't pointed the gun at her. He's been holding out for the right time. Now's the time, apparently.

"Young lady," he says, reaching across his belly with the long barrel pointed at her. She gasps. "Don't be touchin' that."

Nancy snaps her hand into her lap but stares at the gun. This is exactly what Fields was hoping for. But wait, the best part's coming.

He turns into the alley that worked out so well for him and that nice Jap girl. He stops and kills the engine and lights. His long arm grabs the back of her neck and begins pulling her to him as he slides toward the middle of the seat.

Nancy whimpers and says, No, please. He raises the gun.

"I won't tell anyone," she says, crying. "I can't. I can't tell anyone where I was tonight, so I can't tell anyone where I am or what happened. You can do whatever you want. So please just put the gun down."

"You get like you were before, with that young guy."

God, no. She closes her eyes, reaches under her skirt, and begins removing her underwear. For Fields, it's tough enough undoing his pants with one hand, but getting them and his Skivvies past his hard-on is impossible. The gun makes her help him, and there's nothing about it that's less than repulsive. She gets through by closing her eyes.

Then he wants to see her just the way she was, unbuttoned blouse and unsnapped brassiere. She doesn't want to. The gun gets results.

Nancy is quiet as she submits, fighting back each whimper and cry. In some ways, the worst part is opening her eyes from time to time and glancing down, seeing him staring at her while he lifts her up and down, so after a little while she squeezes her eyes shut. He's just fixed on her, like he wants to keep looking at such a pretty picture, and that's why he won't finish. She wishes she could close her ears, too, to keep from hearing him.

Willie Roscoe Fields just cannot understand why she's not making the same kind of happy noises she was fifteen minutes ago. He saw the size of that other guy's dick, so how come she's not loving this twice as much? Plus, he's not wearing no cowboy hat neither, which should feel even better. What gives?

CHAPTER FORTY-THREE

Olson wants to talk to Nancy. John Calgrove says that's impossible. She won't come in. She won't tell anyone what happened. She doesn't want to be connected to this beyond the memory that she knows she'll spend the rest of her life trying to forget. And anyway, he says, she's in enough trouble with her parents just for getting home so late, repeating some cockamamie story he and she had cooked up about their both falling asleep in the boring movie and being there through whatever the other show was and the newsreel and cartoon, too. He says that as far as she's concerned, nothing good can come of her parents hearing what really happened. They won't be protective and loving, and it wouldn't change a thing except how they think of her, which right now isn't very much— though at least this way, she thinks, they'll get over it. But if they knew what really happened and what was happening when it happened and where it happened, then they'd tell her that she deserved what she got. And her father, if not her brother, would kill Calgrove. Yet it was Calgrove who couldn't let this go, even though she begged him to. What happened to her was worse than death, she told him, and if a bus ran her over tomorrow, it would be a blessing. She's suffering. It's obvious to everyone, but the others think she hurts from her parents being mad at her. He's the only one she doesn't have to pretend with, but she won't talk to him, either, worried that her mom or dad or brother will see how they look at each other and wonder why she's crying and whether something more than falling asleep actually happened. Besides, he's leaving for good in a few days—sooner, actually, at the insistence of her father, who blames John for all this.

"And he's right," John says. "It's my fault."

"What's Nancy's last name?" Olson asks yet again. "Where does she live?"

And yet again, he won't break the confidence.

"What kind of gun was it?" she asks.

"I don't know guns," he says.

"How old are you?"

"Twenty?"

"And the girl?"

"Seventeen."

"You said sixteen before."

"I was wrong."

"If she's sixteen, that would be statutory rape."

"Look," he says, "if she was sixteen, would I be here? And what difference does it make if she was nine? She was raped with a gun to her head. Isn't that what's important?"

Olson doesn't believe Calgrove's story. She doesn't know where or how Todd Roark might've hired this guy—maybe he's an actor; maybe Roark's mother knows him—and when she passes this on to Carpenter, it's with the unsolicited opinion that this is all a little bit too convenient to have two alleged rape victims in a row telling the same story and not wanting to give their names. Could also be a copycat doing the same thing that Roark was popped for.

Carpenter surprises her. He says, no, it's not really all that too convenient. It happens, and it couldn't be a copycat because there hasn't been any press to copy from. Though that doesn't mean he's not convinced someone isn't trying to pull something on them.

Danny's furious after following Calgrove outside and speaking privately with him. Calgrove's no faker. Even the great Spencer Tracy couldn't have pulled this off if it were just an act. Calgrove described too many details that only someone who'd lived through it would. The thought of that girl Nancy keeping a terrible secret, and knowing he can't do anything to fix her, makes him want to go back in time to the moment when he should've stopped pretending to play along with Carpenter's madness. That was day one.

"Now he's using a goddamned gun," Danny tells Carpenter. "It's escalating. First he was nice afterward, then he wasn't, then he's pulling a pistol."

"Yeah, that's the story," Carpenter says, emphasizing *story*.

Talking to Olson, Carpenter was talking to someone who believed Roark was behind this, so he wasn't defensive. Talking to Danny, he's talking to the detective who doubted him. "Now we've got two girls who don't want to talk and a gun nobody's claiming."

"So you're still buying that somebody's doing this for Roark?" Danny can't believe it, but he can also tell from his voice that Carpenter's trying to salvage some dignity without flat out admitting that Danny was right. *Is* right.

"I'm not buying, and I'm not selling," Carpenter says. "Right now I don't see anything to change anything."

"We could be heading for murder," Danny says, walking away.

Now what? Danny's not doing it Carpenter's way anymore. Another night driving aimlessly around Central while the guy is somewhere else—assuming Margie's willing to spend the time with him—is plain stupid. Forget Carpenter. He'll take it up with the captain. So what if

Lohrman and Carpenter have history together and Carpenter brings up Margie? Danny's sure that at this point what's happening on the street trumps everything else. But that doesn't mean he wants Carpenter to see him walking into Lohrman's office. So first he runs downstairs to Roark's cell and brings him up-to-date.

"A gun," Roark mutters. "Got a goddamn gun. Jesus."

"You sure you don't want out?" Danny says. He's worried about the eye. From the looks of things, Roark might lose it if he doesn't see a doctor soon.

"You know and I know that the next time this guy pulls something," Roark says, "my house is the first stop. And if I'm on the street, I won't even see the bullet."

"You could leave town," Danny says.

"I ain't leaving town. You could watch me get on the train, but unless you got a camera on me twenty-four hours a day at the Statue of Liberty, they just gonna think I slipped back into town anyway."

Danny doesn't have to ask where Roark got these ideas. He got them from the cops assigned as guards. Negroes accused of raping white women face it all the time, and that he was once a cop, too—even if they never let him feel that way at the time—just makes tormenting and threatening him that much more fun. Still, the eye issue aside, he's right to stay put till the bad guy takes his place.

Alone with Lohrman, Danny lays it all out—everything except how he actually feels about the woman who helped him try to find the rapist—and in not so many words asks to be made lead detective on the case and given the resources to form a task force.

In not so many words, Lohrman tells him soon, not yet, we'll see what happens—as if cutting the baby in half would satisfy both mothers. He's no Solomon, that's for sure.

"We're talking about a real bad actor, Captain," Danny insists.

Lohrman knows what's right, but sometimes there are other considerations.

Danny understands just what he means because right now he has to consider what might happen if he goes over Lohrman's head to an inspector—Hugh Farnham, for example. Or even the chief himself. If he does, he'd better have a plan in mind before walking in, and the plan better work.

He spends the night by himself, doing just what he said he wasn't going to do—driving around looking for this guy.

But now he's thinking as much as looking.

CHAPTER FORTY-FOUR

Willie Roscoe Fields likes the Ardmore at Fifteenth Street location. Twice it's been blessed for him, maybe because the corner is the parking lot of a Catholic school, and driving up he always asks for his prayers to be answered. So far, they have. Tonight looks like they will, too.

Fields parks on the street and takes the tools of his trade from the glove box and feels to make sure the gun is where it's supposed to be; best buy he ever made. He eyes his target. A jalopy is in the corner of the lot, which means inside either some Negroes are necking, and he knows that ain't happening in this part of town—and if it is, he'll beat it out of there—or some really young white kids.

Close enough. They're two Mexicans, he finds out when he sneaks up on them. Mexican girls are nice, he's learned.

Ramona Ortiz is twenty and on the verge of tears when he identifies himself as a plainclothes vice officer there to take them in and orders them out of the car. Oscar Escobar, who was halfway to home plate when the knock came on the window, is twenty-three and grew up in Boyle Heights getting in fights every day. He knows how to handle himself with his fists and knows he could take this big Negro down if it weren't for the gun. Bullshit that he's a cop. They're being rolled, that's for sure, and he can only hope that Ramona's smart enough not to believe what he can't tell her out loud not to believe without risking a bullet from this crazy *vato*.

She's not. She's still there, still thinking she's going to jail, after Fields circled back after ordering Escobar out of the car at Washington and Union after enjoying that a gun can make someone who doesn't want to shut up shut up and doesn't want to get out get out. At work in the morning, Fields is going to have to thank Darryl for the excellent merchandise.

Yep, Mexican girls with guns to their heads are nice.

CHAPTER FORTY-FIVE

Ramona Ortiz and Oscar Escobar are not actors. They're not making up anything. Even Olson believes that now. And Carpenter has to admit it out loud. He doesn't actually come out and say that the guy in the cell downstairs isn't their man, but he does more listening than talking while Danny coaxes every detail out of the couple who were in the wrong place, handing the girl Kleenexes as needed. Only later does it occur to Danny that maybe Carpenter might've been so quiet because he felt out of his element, what with the Mexican detective interviewing two Mexes. But no, it was real. Carpenter's got his detective's brain and vision back, and he's contrite enough to want to do his job now, and that's how you do your job when your partner's doing his so well. You shut up and listen for clues that might help you help him solve this thing.

"Got any ideas?" Carpenter asks. He's not the type to ask if he didn't mean it. This is as close to an *I'm sorry* as he's going to offer, and Danny doesn't need anything more. What he wants is a free hand and the resources to wrap this thing up fast.

"Yeah, actually I do," Danny says. "But first I have to go make sure I can pull it off before we pitch it."

We. Danny wonders if Carpenter caught that.

He did.

CHAPTER FORTY-SIX

Once the guard lets you on to the Universal-International lot, you can pretty much wander where you like, if you like that sort of thing. Danny does. He just doesn't want to be too obvious about it. After all, he's on official police business. But even cops enjoy what goes on behind the screen. Actually, some cops are the most starstruck. The motorcycle-patrol guys fight for the off-duty duty guarding location sets; it's extra pay and sometimes the actors come over to say hello and make sure word gets out that they're regular folk who deserve a pass if they happen to drive too fast or drunk.

Danny thinks that Margie would get a kick out of this. He takes the long way around the lot to the offices of Mark VII Limited, Jack Webb's company that produces *Dragnet,* a couple of hundred yards from the soundstages where it's shot. The show knocks off for lunch at twelve thirty, and he doesn't want to disturb Mr. Webb on set, so he'll kill time with a little stargazing. Sometimes there's nothing much to see, and sometimes there is. Today's not bad. He sees that fat director who's on TV with scary shows getting into a limousine outside a soundstage. He sees

Rock Hudson and Lauren Bacall walking and tries not to stare at Lauren Bacall but it's hard. He sees Esther Williams in regular clothes instead of a bathing suit and passes a set made to look like Kiddieland. In fact, it says KIDDIELAND, and Abbott and Costello play the guys who run it. How funny. He'll have to take Margie when it comes out.

Webb's not at all stiff, the way he is playing Joe Friday. He welcomes Danny like an old friend into his office with a couch bigger than Danny's living room and asks him to join him for lunch in the commissary. Danny says thanks but no thanks, he has to get back to work, and what that work is "depends on what you tell me" when he begs a favor.

Danny's positive Webb will say yes. Anything good for L.A. and the LAPD is good for Webb. That's more or less the deal Webb struck with Parker. The only question in Webb's mind might be why Parker himself or one of his inspectors didn't call for whatever this is. If Webb didn't already look so intrigued, Danny would make sure to work in right up front that Parker and his inspectors don't know yet.

"Let's hear it," Webb says, leaning forward across his desk.

Danny lays out the whole story, even hinting at the budding romance with Margie, which brings a smile. But he focuses on the shattered girls and the innocent man sitting in a jail cell who again this morning—and here Danny has to be a little careful not to reveal too much about the department's role—told Danny that he intends to stay put till the bad guy's off the street.

"That's a hell of a story," Webb says. "And you know what? Hitchcock is shooting something like that."

"I just saw him," Danny says.

"Maybe checking on his show. The movie's being shot at Warners. Henry Fonda. It's about an innocent man who police think is guilty, and the more he tries to prove he's innocent, the more guilty they think he is. He goes all the way to trial and prison. True story. I read it in *Life*."

"Yeah, I think I did, too," Danny says. "Doesn't end well."

Even if that's not quite true—because the man is eventually cleared—this is the best setup line Webb has had all day. "Well, we'll have to have a happy ending here," he says. "Whatever I can do."

Danny tells him what he can do. He can make a phone call.

CHAPTER FORTY-SEVEN

They would've held the meeting in Lohrman's office if there were places for everyone to sit. Instead, they moved it to Inspector Farnsworth's. There's Lohrman, Farnsworth, another inspector named McQuown, Carpenter, and Danny. Farnsworth is the senior officer. Danny has the floor. He's already made clear that the only way to catch this guy is by getting wherever he's going before he gets there. Danny's already promised something good, already been named head of this ad hoc task force, already been given a blank check for whatever resources he needs. And now he's explaining his idea, knowing that if it's not as good as they think it has to be, none of the other stuff is true anymore.

Danny's idea is to borrow a dozen patrol cops from their regular duty and pair them with plainclothesmen, putting each couple in unmarked cars from midnight to four at lovers' lanes he's already chosen. They'll pretend to be making out, and sooner or later the bad guy will come to the right place and pick on the wrong car.

"Wait a second, Danny, we don't have enough girl cops to pull that off," Farnsworth says, imagining two guys with 3:00 A.M. shadows; not exactly enticing bait.

"We don't need them," Danny says. "We'll make the men look like ladies."

He says he's already sealed the deal with the studio. For as many nights as necessary, the makeup wizards at Universal-International will take care of the faces, and the wardrobe department will do the rest. All the cops have to bring are their guns and know-how. By the time the rapist gets close enough to say never mind, it'll be too late.

The others are silent now. No reaction. That's a good sign, not to get an immediate no.

Farnsworth doesn't even have to look at the others. "How long before you can get your team out there?" he asks.

CHAPTER FORTY-EIGHT

Willie Roscoe Fields is driving east on Adams. It's late. He's tired. True, he's never too tired to make love, and do it twice, but he's not even looking tonight. Tomorrow night for sure. No, now he's on his way home from Club Casino, with Johnny Magnus on the radio selling something besides himself between songs. "Ladies, you can chat about the rage— and you know what I mean by *rage*—for the horsetail hairdo. So, if you don't have the real stuff, then drop over to Lessie Stevenson's Human Hair Salon, located at 1228 West Jefferson, and tell Lessie to get you right in style for those crisp summer days still ahead of us."

Fields does not like the thought of a horsetail on a girl's head, and if a girl wore one, he wouldn't make love to her till she took it off.

Wait, forget the hair. Here comes the song of songs.

"Never know how much I love you . . ."

Unbelievable. Just what he was wanting to hear. Just what he's always wanting to hear, and it's on just because he wanted to hear it. Or so it seems. He sings along, hitting every note sweet, pounding out the beat with his hands on the wheel.

This is the best time ever for Willie Roscoe Fields. He's never before gotten everything so fast and easy, like life is a restaurant menu and he can order up whatever he wants and there it'll be. *Lemme see here. I'll have one of those and one of those and one of those.*

"I get a fever that's so hard to bear . . ."

Uh-oh, what's that?

What it is, is a pretty Negro girl, eighteen or nineteen, in an orange-and-white waitress uniform, like a delicious Creamsicle, sitting on a bus bench just past Arlington. Fields glances around. The wide streets are almost empty.

He pulls up in front of her and leans over to roll down the passenger window.

"Wanna ride, young lady?" he asks.

"No thank you," she says. "I'm waiting for my boyfriend. He'll be here any minute."

"Suit yourself," he says, driving away.

Three minutes later when he comes back, the passenger window is up again.

He again leans over to roll it down. She's smart to be afraid and dumb not to run. She knows better. She was taught better. But she never thought she'd have to use what she learned, even at one in the morning on a desolate city street.

"Who's your boyfriend?" he asks.

"Why?"

Fields turns the flashlight on and holds the beam over the sheriff's badge. "Do you know who I am?"

"No."

"Plainclothes vice officer. Come here and show me your ID."

"I don't have any," she says.

"You know, girl, I'm gonna have to take you in, as you fit the 'scription of a girl who stoled a wallet off a man a little while ago. Get here in the car."

She does, opening the door and sitting down.

"Give me your purse and let me look inside."

She hands it to him. He tosses it over his shoulder into the backseat.

"Hey," she says as he jams the car into first and screeches away from the curb, the acceleration closing her door. He turns down Arlington. "What're you doing? Where we going?"

"Girl, you goin' to jail," he says. "I just told you that."

Her name is Josephine Johnson. She's nineteen. Scared shitless. And that's before she knows the half of it.

Fields turns onto Twenty-sixth Place and stops half a block down, under a broken streetlamp. Engine and lights off.

"Where's the police station?" she says.

The answer is the gun in his right hand to her head. She screams till he presses it harder into her temple. "Don't holler," he says.

Once again, the gun gets results.

"Okay," she mutters, and nods.

That doesn't mean he lessens the pressure against her head.

"Good. It's nitty-gritty time."

His left hand unbuckles his belt, unclasps his pants, and lowers his zipper. Josephine tries not to look, but there it is. By the time Fields unpacks himself, he's at full mast. He looks over at her like this is show-and-tell and he's damned proud of what he brought to show. Tomorrow the girl can tell all her friends—tell them how she gave this man she just met a blow job he'll never forget.

Something about this is deeply, abysmally foul—performing this act on a stranger against your will with a gun to your head in the front seat of the stranger's car in the middle of night and the world sleeping outside not caring anything about you.

Had Willie Fields been paying attention, he might have heard Josephine Johnson's sobs. True, they were muffled by her choking sounds, but he might've heard them—not that he would've cared—if he hadn't been babbling so much about how good it felt and how he liked it, all the while holding the gun against her bobbing head.

This goes on forever before Fields gets there with a loud groan, so he also misses the puking noise when she throws up on his lap. She didn't mean to; it just happened. She gagged and that was that. In some ways, she's as stunned as he is. She even says, "I'm sorry."

Fields can't believe it. It takes him a second to register that the employees' all-you-can-eat-free dinner of mashed potatoes with gravy and carrots and macaroni with cheese from Dinah's Kitchen is now all over his lap.

"Shit, girl!" he says, lifting his pants and Skivvies away from his skin.

That means his hands are free. The gun must be somewhere else.

"Shit," he says. "Damn."

Josephine jams the door handle open and runs out onto the sidewalk. She's still running when she hears the car start, which she takes as her cue to run back close enough to get his license-plate numbers before he patches out and out of sight.

Smart girl.

CHAPTER FORTY-NINE

Danny and Carpenter drive to the Seventy-seventh station to interview Josephine Johnson in person. The desk sergeant called them when she came in. He knew to do that because of the officers he'd been told he'll be losing to special duty until they catch the guy—four of them from Seventy-seventh. What's going on is a big deal, and it wouldn't be bad to be part of it somehow. He wishes he could himself instead of Rechsteiner, Starkey, Kohn, and Kennedy. Not that he's dying to put on mascara and Pan-Cake makeup over a dress, but it might be a hoot.

The first thing Danny does is thank Josephine Johnson for getting the license plate, even though it wasn't quite the big break that it might've been. The DeSoto is registered to a Mr. James Lonnon at a boardinghouse address where no one's seen him for at least a year, but, yeah, the sketch is a good likeness. Danny then ran Lonnon's name and came up with nothing, no record. He suspects it's a pseudonym; there's no way to cross-check it against legal names on rap sheets.

After listening to Josephine Johnson, Danny's sure that this Lonnon or whoever is losing any sense of reality he may have had. Last night was a Tuesday, not a weekend, and last night was the first time he hadn't set out to find someone in a lovers' lane. This was a crime of opportunity, meaning he was going somewhere else, probably home, and there she was. He took advantage. But even if he did, it means he's driving around with that gun all the time, and who knows what opportunities will be out there tomorrow and the next day? Does it mean that he's changing his MO? Danny hopes not. He has a plan that can work, but only for the MO the guy had been using. What Danny doesn't have is enough resources to set up decoys all over the city and send unmarked cars to prowl dark streets, hoping to catch a fish jumping out of the pond. At least with the lovers' lanes, a dozen decoy cars can cover the likeliest spots.

Danny could use another night to work through the details. Almost thirty people are involved now, more if you count everyone at Universal. And one more than that if you count Carpenter, who at this point agrees to just stand there and watch until they bring in the guy—*if* they bring him in. Carpenter's too old to pretend to be necking as a man, and with a wig, lipstick, and makeup on, he'd look like Frankenstein, which, come to think of it, was shot at Universal.

It's noon. If they're going to get out there tonight, he's got about twelve hours left to finish picking the right guys, work out the logistics, arrange the temporary reassignments, meet and rehearse, hand out the locations. This isn't a pre-mission briefing during the war, when everyone already knew his job and all that needed discussing was the target and angle of attack. This is a lot to do, making sure policemen who've never before done something like this don't tip off the night prowler that they're onto him.

No, there's not enough time to get out there right away. That's not a tragedy. The odds say the guy won't try to pull something again tonight, the second straight night, unless he really is changing his MO, in which case the undercover stakeout is doomed no matter what.

While logic says the plan doesn't have to execute perfectly its first night out, as long as it's perfect the night the bad guy meets the good guys, Danny wants it perfect every night. He knows they have only one shot at this.

CHAPTER FIFTY

Fields gags a little when he climbs in his car for the drive to work. That sour vomit smell. Where's it coming from? He already threw his trousers in the incinerator, and the girl's purse, too, after first rummaging through and taking her $6.73—probably her tips last night. She wasn't lying, neither. She really didn't have ID.

He liked her. If he knew her name, he wouldn't mind seeing her again. But not if she's going to puke like that every time, and he sure doesn't want to keep smelling her like this. He rolls down the windows on his way to work and leaves them down until lunch, when he wipes the seat and the floor with solvent. It's not good for the upholstery, but so what if it works.

About the time he decides he's satisfied with the cleaning and won't have to sell the car, a *California Eagle* reporter is polishing the story she just finished writing about Josephine Johnson. The reporter copied the info off the police blotter, saw it was a Negro perpetrator and a Negro victim and that the crime took place in a Negro neighborhood, and now she had herself a front-page story.

The reporter files her story just about the moment Dorothea Foster shows up in the *Eagle* offices on East Forty-third Place and Central to hand this week's *Dot's Dashes* column to the paper's editor, Loren Miller. Dorothea, who has a debutante daughter about Josephine's age, reads the article, shakes her head, decries what's happening to her little piece of heaven, and wonders how much longer till the thugs drive out all the Negroes interested in high society and life's finer things.

If only Willie Roscoe Fields knew that Dorothea Foster has noticed him. He'd be proud.

CHAPTER FIFTY-ONE

A reporter named Donna Pree had phoned the LAPD public information officer for comment about what had happened to Josephine Johnson, and word reached Danny that the *Eagle* had an article in the works.

Off the record, Danny phoned the paper's offices and tried to talk the editor into holding it till next week, by which time, he said, he hoped to have caught the guy—who, if he saw the piece, might go underground, which would undermine the complicated operation Danny was putting in place to nab him.

Well, that was the wrong thing to say to a newspaperman. It told Loren Miller that this rapist was connected to something other than an ordinary 288 or 261, even a 207, depending on how it was charged. What about that? What else had the guy done that merited such detailed goings-on? Danny insisted he wasn't at liberty to disclose any more information but then had to concede Miller's point that residents of the area needed to be warned about a pervert driving around looking for easy prey.

Now, reading Donna Pree's story, Danny remembers from his Black

Dahlia days how much more careful you have to be answering reporters than you do interrogating criminals.

Headlined POLICE SEEK SEX MANIAC, the story showed some real initiative and quoted sources that Miller or Pree must've tapped after learning this was a bigger deal than first believed. "An all-points bulletin," it began, "has been issued by the police department for the capture of a sex pervert, kidnaper and robber who, posing as a deputy sheriff, has been kidnapping women in the West Adams and Wilshire districts for the last three weeks."

The report continued on for several more paragraphs, but this being a family newspaper, propriety required the omission of what precisely the bad guy had done to Josephine Johnson. It wasn't propriety, however, that explained not publishing a description of the perpetrator or his car, both of which were available to Miss Pree. No, this had been an implicit recognition that, even in that part of town, even white policemen sometimes have to be trusted to do their jobs in the dark—as long as when the job's finally done what happened in the dark can withstand sunlight. The irony isn't lost on Danny that this sort of story might have ended the saga had it run over a month ago, before the gun. Now, who knows? You can't blame the *Eagle* for not knowing to leave out the part about West Adams and Wilshire, where Danny's men will be staked out in a dozen spots.

Oh, well. All Danny can do is carry out the plan and hope that the big fish is hungry enough to take the bait knowing someone's trying to catch him.

CHAPTER FIFTY-TWO

As usual, at lunch on Friday Willie Fields is sitting alone on his power buggy, eating the greasy burger with fixings he bought that morning, which is no less tasty for now being cold. What distracts him from day-dreaming is Darryl and the guys across the backyard, laughing. They do that a lot. But this is different. They're laughing at Blue, who's holding a copy of the new *Eagle* and reading something in a pretend girl's sexy voice: " 'Lonely? If you have friends from out of town who desire a dinner companion, theater date, et cetera, or if you are interested in meeting a sparkling acquaintance, contact Miss Kay Williams Escort Services between the hours of one p.m. and nine p.m.' "

Fields walks over, laughs with them, says, "Do it again," which surprises them.

But then they spot that look on his face. God almighty, as little as a phony girl's voice and sucker's ad are enough to stiff up this fellow. Still, it's good to share the laugh with him. Maybe it's a start on some camaraderie. Maybe they'll ask him along to see Fats Domino and Clyde McPhatter playing the blues jubilee at the Shrine.

To accommodate Fields, Blue reads the ad again, exaggerating even more the girlie voice and innuendo.

When the laughter dies down, Fields asks to see the ad. Blue hands him the paper. Fields hopes the number to call isn't an Axminster. Good, it's a Republic. He can pronounce that. He'll have to buy a copy. Darryl says go ahead, keep it—"If you tell us what she really looks like."

The guys erupt. Fields doesn't know why, but he smiles and shrugs before walking back to the buggy and his lunch. He spreads the *Eagle* on his lap and begins reading a story with a headline that's right up his alley. *Wait. Huh?*

He's so surprised when he finally figures out that—*Damn!*—this is about him, he drops his burger. Damn, he can still eat it but the grease and mustard are murder on the paper. He can't read a thing.

At quitting time, Fields is so excited he doesn't even deposit his pay-check before stopping at Goldilocks Liquors and buying five copies of the *Eagle*. That's five more than he's bought in the last year, and these are all the same paper. Fields wonders whether the clerk wonders why he's buying five. He hopes so. While he's there, he picks up a bottle of Scoresby's.

At home, he arranges the stack of papers in a tight bundle on his dresser. He wishes he'd bought six, so he'd still have five clean copies after wrinkling the one he read in the car. And read again on the street out front. And reads again and again on his bed, then once or twice in the backyard. He can't believe he made the paper. He's never had a write-up before, and, man, he wants to brag in the worst way that this "sex maniac" is him.

Should he tell Mrs. Terrell, if she walks out and sees him reading? He rehearses: *What that you reading, Willie? It's the new* Eagle, *just came out yesterday, full o' interestin' stories. Oh, like what? Well, like, uh, like about a fun'ral for a gospel singer got executed in Atlanta for rapin' a white woman, and, uh, well, a sex maniac kidnapping women*

in West Adams and Wilshire for the last three weeks. Man, longer than
that—and how they know 'bout those other things, too?

Fields reads the story again. Okay, so that girl's name was Josephine
Johnson. And there's her address on West Thirty-ninth. Yeah, he knows
right where that is. Maybe he'll drop by sometime. Say hi.

CHAPTER FIFTY-THREE

It's not the waiting night after night, midnight to four, then grabbing a few fitful hours of sleep that bother Danny Galindo. It's his nagging suspicion that the rapist saw the *Eagle* article and disappeared—or, worse, has taken to haunting new grounds outside West Adams and Wilshire, where victims may be even less willing to report being raped by a "huge Negro" with a gun at their head.

The worry that he and his guys are badly located keeps getting worse. They feel it, too. He can tell. Morale is letting down. No wonder. Those first few nights at the studio were a kick, having professionals pick out wigs and dresses to wear over their street clothes and slathering mascara and lipstick on them and then looking in the mirror. Lots of laughs and mugging. They all fought so hard to do it that they finally agreed to alternate. But eight long nights on, they're either dreading their turn tomorrow or wishing it's not theirs tonight.

Danny doesn't have to do that part. He's the only one with a live female. Olson volunteered for the job but Danny turned her down, and she didn't have to ask why. Doris Hall works juvenile at Hollywood division and looks like she came out of central casting for a young lady stopping off to thank her boyfriend after a double feature and supper. Maybe that's one reason morale is sinking. The other guys bitch about Danny sitting with his arm around Doris all night while they're stuck with Old Pig Breath or Booger Face. For about three one-hundredths of a second last week, Danny considered asking Farnham to sign off on Margie as his partner instead of this licensed cop who can hit a firing-range target. No offense to Doris, but juvie in Hollywood tracking down stolen hubcaps isn't where you're going to make any bones. If anything does happen on this stakeout, he's not sure he can count on her to perform any better than Margie might have.

Every night before leaving for the stakeout, Danny checks on Roark. Then he drives home and calls Margie. In private he can say more than there's nothing to tell her, other than that thing that he can't really tell her. Yet.

So that the cops can communicate on stakeout, each of their cars has a walkie-talkie—perfect for calling the play-by-play of what regular couples, most of them teens, are doing in adjacent cars, with some of them going all the way. But even that gets old after a while, especially knowing you could be busting them for doing what you'd much rather be doing if you weren't on stakeout. The whole thing's a drain. You can tell how late it is every night by the reactions to an occasional seat-ripping fart over the airwaves. Just before four, it really has to be something special to get a laugh. Even from Doris.

She and Danny are parked in his Ford on South Hobart, halfway between Pico and Washington. Twinkling lights? Check. Darkness? Check. Privacy? Check. That's why this spot gets its share of action. Same with the cemetery lot not far to the south and east, and half a dozen more sites in a ten-mile radius. Danny didn't pick the assignments based on anything other than chance, including his own. He doesn't believe his spot is where their guy is most likely to hit. It's just one of the twelve, all of them as likely as the others—assuming the guy is going to hit at all. And right now, all assumptions are off. This being a Saturday night—and the second Saturday night they've done this—if the guy doesn't hit tonight, Danny's going to rethink his whole scheme. Farnham won't have to call him in. He'll call himself in. Which reminds Danny that Carpenter's probably loving that absolutely fucking nothing is happening and that Roark is still locked up, refusing to come out, which seems wiser every day. Carpenter visited Roark and said he wouldn't mind if Roark got out, but Roark could see he didn't mean it, and now cops are again whispering about what an amazing coincidence it is that all of a sudden nobody's showing up to claim that a "huge Negro" with a badge raped and kidnapped them.

Those first few hours in the car with Doris, Roark was pretty much all Danny talked about. Then he might've spent a little too much time talking about Margie's role in this, and maybe Doris noticed. Then they talked about Doris a bit, then some about Danny, then about the couples in the next cars, which was uncomfortable until they got used to it, and now they don't really have anything useful to talk about.

In Danny's mind, he'll never run out of useful things to say with Margie.

CHAPTER FIFTY-FOUR

Willie Roscoe Fields feels better now. Back in action. After he read his article in the paper he drank a lot too much and visited some clubs, and when things weren't going so well he fought the urge to tell the girls he was the guy written about in the paper he kept in his pocket across from his gun. By the time he made it home that night he felt so bad he had to stay in bed two days, and since then has kept a low profile. Just in case they're still looking for him.

Tonight's Saturday, though. It's been ten days since a woman last loved him, the longest he's gone since he can't remember. No way he's going home till he meets someone new.

CHAPTER FIFTY-FIVE

Danny checks his watch. Three o'clock. He's been in a mood all night, wracking his brain for what to do tomorrow after four o'clock comes and goes tonight.

"Look," Doris whispers, pointing behind them to the corner of Fifteenth Street. A car with its lights off that could be a DeSoto has parked, and between the car and a tree is a man. "See him?"

Danny's right arm is around her shoulder, so he has to twist to his right without being noticed. The windows are cracked to keep the car from fogging, which means they can be seen, too. He pulls her closer and pretends to kiss her, covering the move. Is it really what she says it is? Danny's not sure his eyes aren't showing him what he wants to see, like a desert mirage. No, yes, absolutely. It's a man. A Negro. Huge, too. And he keeps peeking out from behind the tree, gauging when to make his move. Theirs is the only other car around now. Danny presses the walkie-talkie with his left hand: "Stand by," he says. "This may be it."

For five minutes nothing happens. "I think we're going to have to look like we're really going at it," Danny says.

"Okay," Doris says.

Danny readjusts the mini-nightstick on his right hip and pushes her down onto her back across the front seat, then pretends to climb on top of her, his backside pumping gently as he watches out the back window through his periphery.

He was right. That does it. The figure creeps from behind the tree and begins crawling toward them. He's about twenty-five yards away. Danny wonders if that's a flashlight or a gun. It's a gun.

In a whisper, Danny tells Doris to alert the other units, eases his revolver from its holster, quickly reaches back, opens the passenger door, and jumps from the car.

"Police," he yells. "Stop right there. Don't move."

Danny grips his revolver with two hands away from his body, muzzle pointed at Fields, no misunderstanding the intent in his voice or posture.

"Okay," Fields says. "Don't shoot." But he doesn't stop. He stands and raises the Luger.

Danny fires. Misses. Fires again. This one hits Fields in the thigh. Danny hears the little shriek and sees the leg buckle.

"Get the handcuffs," Danny calls to Doris.

He glances her way, and in that moment Fields takes off running east along Fifteenth toward Harvard. Danny aims, changes his mind, and gives chase instead. If this guy's really hit in the thigh, he must be Superman.

Just the other side of Harvard, Danny runs him down into a horseshoe courtyard of attached apartments. Danny knows he's in there. Where, though? From what he can see, the way in is the only way out. Danny really should wait for backup, but how's he supposed to call for it? No, it's just him and this guy. They both have guns. This is stupid. He could easily get killed, and if he fires and misses, the bullet might go through a wall and kill someone else. The right thing is to duck out of the pale streetlight and guard to make sure the guy doesn't escape before help comes, but help may not be coming and dawn is an hour away. Besides, there's enough adrenaline pumping through him that Danny feels like Superman himself—and right now he'd rather die than let this bastard get away.

Danny's on 360-degree high alert, gun raised, taking long, cool, quiet steps into the courtyard, eyes scanning the darkness and shadows. "I'm a police officer," he says. "Put down your gun and come out."

Danny recognizes the sound of a trigger being squeezed. He winces but there's no report, no muzzle flash.

Again comes the trigger click, harder this time. Still nothing. Danny realizes he doesn't need to wince. If he can hear the click, he's not dead. Bullets fly faster than sound.

He inches toward it—and is pounced on by a giant man flying from the shadows.

Before Danny can shoot, and at this range he would have, Fields grabs Danny in a bear hug. At first two arms are necessary to pin Danny's arms to his side, then only one long, muscular arm does the job. The guy has eight or nine inches on him and almost a hundred pounds. Danny can smell alcohol on his breath and see the gun in his right hand. Luger. Danny remembers seeing German soldiers with them. Fields presses its muzzle above Danny's right ear and again squeezes. Click. Nothing, still alive. Danny figures the guy's got .38 ammo in the clip instead of 9 mm; common mistake, but sometimes the bullet chambers anyway and fires.

Enraged, Fields yelps like an animal and squeezes both arms tight around Danny's chest, trying to pulverize him, then with another howl shakes him up and down like a piston. Danny's revolver drops from his hand to the ground. Whoever gets it first ends the fight.

The way the guy's arms are pinned across Danny's biceps, Danny can wiggle his right hand and reach the short nightstick in his back pocket. He has just enough leverage to maneuver it forward and, with a short, powerful wrist flick, whack the guy's forearm. Twice. It's working. The guy's grip loosens. A third whack breaks it.

Danny's exhausted from fighting, panting and out of breath, but has to grab his gun. Before he can, instinct tells him to turn, which he does just in time to block the guy from pistol-whipping him with the Luger.

Even beneath the soft lamplight, Danny has a clear view of the man's face and wonders how anyone mistook him for Todd Roark.

Fields breathes in hard, short, fast spurts, an angry bull, maybe from the thigh wound. Danny can see blood leaking.

A glint of something flashes in Fields's eyes. Fear? Confusion? Pain? Madness? Danny doesn't know.

They maneuver around each other like it's a knife fight. Danny's gun lies on the walkway behind him. He can't bend for it without the Luger smashing his skull, and he can't let this guy close enough or he'll pick it up himself and fire. Danny has one second to decide whether he can dive, grab, roll, aim, and shoot before something bad happens, but decides he can't. So he kicks the revolver along the concrete toward the back of the courtyard. Now it's lost in the shadows, invisible to both of them.

It's come down to Danny and his smarts and his nightstick against Fields and his size and his Luger that may not ever fire.

Light suddenly floods from an uncovered hundred-watt bulb on the porch of the back unit. Its door opens and a lady in curlers asks what's going on.

"Get back inside," Danny shouts. "I'm a cop, call the cops."

She slams the door but the light's still on. Both men can see where Danny's gun is. Danny has no choice; he has to break for it. And the second he does, Fields sprints down Harvard.

By the time Danny picks up his .38 and reaches the street, there's no sign of the guy. Danny runs the direction he saw him go, checking east and west on Fifteenth before continuing on Harvard. After another block, he stops to rest, hands on knees. Gone.

Shit.

Since the war, this is the closest he's come to being dead. And all he feels is mad. At himself.

He runs back toward his car. It's still there, and so is Doris Hall.

But not the DeSoto.

"Where'd he go?" Danny asks.

She points west and says, "He had a gun. I called it in."

Shit.

Here come the sirens, louder and closer.

Danny picks up the walkie-talkie and tells the others what happened and where, says they should join all the other units cruising for the DeSoto.

"Hang on," says Houtchens. He's the one wearing lipstick tonight, parked with Dettrow in a spot on Sixteenth and St. Andrews that this guy hit once before. "I think we've got company."

"You have to be kidding me," Danny says. He starts up his car. "We're on our way."

You gotta be kidding me.

CHAPTER FIFTY-SIX

For Willie Roscoe Fields, the night is young. When he needs a woman, he needs a woman, and he's not going home without having a woman.

He drove west on Fifteenth and is heading south on St. Andrews to Sixteenth. That place has been lucky for him. Twice.

He stares at his thigh, bleeding on the seat that he cleaned so nice of that puke. He doesn't care. Doesn't even feel it. The gun's in his lap. He's going to have to talk to Darryl tomorrow about how come the thing wouldn't fire. Piece of junk. He tosses it out the window and then says *fuck*, because the thing doesn't actually have to fire to make girls love him easier. Don't matter anyway, as long as he's got his badge and flashlight.

Well, looks like this place is still lucky. Four o'clock in the a of m, and there's still poon to be had in that Dodge, a couple getting it on. Now's his turn.

He parks behind the tree, kills the engine and lights, and peeks out from the trunk before making his move. He's ready now, and too tired to crawl. They're busy anyway. They won't notice him till it's too late.

But it is too late.

Houtchens and Dettrow spring from the car, one out each door, guns raised. "Police," says Houtchens.

Fields can't believe what he sees—a man dressed like a lady pointing a gun at him. He turns and runs, and the two cops take aim just as four cars converge from down St. Andrews and across Fifteenth, one of them Danny's. In a moment, seven guns are aimed at Willie Roscoe Fields, one of them Danny's.

"You going to make us kill you?" Danny asks.

Fields finally puts up his hands, not understanding why so many men are in drag.

"Show me your palms," Danny says.

Fields unclenches his fists. From the right one drops the sheriff's badge.

CHAPTER FIFTY-SEVEN

While Fields was being bandaged, Danny went down to see Todd Roark. Actually, he went down to open the jail door. It's not supposed to happen like this; the charges have to be dropped by the DA. But that's just a formality now, and after the night he's had—and the month Roark's had—no one says squat.

Danny's glad Roark knows he doesn't have to say thank-you, because then Danny would have to say I'm sorry for letting this go on so long.

Something else that's not supposed to happen happens when Danny brings Roark into the interview room with him, where Roark was last time. And where Carpenter already is now with Fields, at Danny's request.

Carpenter's shaking his head at something Fields has just told him, then sees Roark but doesn't make any more of it than that. Neither does Roark. He glances at Carpenter about a second before staring at Fields with so much hate he almost trembles. The only one who can't see that is Fields. It would be all right with Carpenter if Roark meted out a little justice, Carpenter's way of trying to square things. But Roark's being there to see this is gift enough, and Danny's the one to honor.

"I've been talking to Mr. Willie Roscoe Fields here," says Carpenter. "Mr. Fields, why don't you tell these two gentlemen what you just told me."

"I said," says Fields, "that those girls were all girlfriends of mine."

"How many girlfriends are we talking about?" Danny asks.

The answer is what Danny knew and feared but not what he wants to hear. There were a lot more rapes than reports.

Eventually, Willie Roscoe Fields gets around to admitting that the gun sometimes helped these girls to make up their minds that they were his friends, and sometimes he had other ways of persuading them.

"Is that the gun you tried to kill me with?" Danny asks.

"Oh, I wouldn't try nothing like that," Fields says.

"Where's the gun now?"

"Don't know."

Fields tells them everything else, though. It's seven thirty when he's led back to a cell, and fatigue is starting to catch up to Danny. He knows they need the gun. Carpenter says out loud what's true, that because of the false ID's by the other victims, the best charge they have on him is attempted murder of a police officer. What a goddamned irony that is.

Roark asks if he can use Danny's phone and begins dialing. "Mama," he says, cupping a hand over his bad eye, "it's over. . . . Yes, thank God. . . . Yes, I know today is Teri Denise's birthday. Two years old. Mama, can you help me find her? I need to see her."

Danny doesn't want to overhear any more, and Carpenter walks into the kitchen so he doesn't have to.

Roark is still on the phone a minute later when a uniform leads a nine-year-old boy through the maze of desks to where Danny's leaning back in a chair. The boy is holding a pencil poked through the trigger guard of a gun. A Luger.

"This is just how he walked in, Detective," the uniform says. "Swear to God. "Go ahead, tell the detective what you told me."

"I was walking to summer school," the boy says, "and I saw the gun in the gutter."

"How'd you know to pick it up that way?" Danny asks.

"From *Dragnet*."

CHAPTER FIFTY-EIGHT

Now it's Danny's turn to make a call. Later he'll notify all the victims, ask them to come down and confirm that it was this convicted rapist and parole jumper who'd assaulted them. He knows they will, and he can imagine how horrible they'll feel when they realize their mistake. But right now there's only one person he wants to talk to, and as far as he's concerned, everybody else can damn well hear what he has to say. He dials and in a loud voice asks for Margie, hoping like hell she hasn't left for work yet.

She hasn't.

"Good morning," he says. "Doing anything for breakfast?"

CHAPTER FIFTY-NINE

RAPIST TELLS TALE OF NIGHT PROWLING

By Donna Pree

Willie Roscoe Fields, tall and good-looking, who faces possible death in San Quentin's gas chamber, in a special interview in county jail, told the Eagle Tuesday the circumstances that had started him out as a night-time prowler . . . .

"The day of my arrest when I walked up to Officer Galindo's car, I admit I had a gun. I walked about 10 feet from the car and he told me to drop my gun or he'd shoot to kill. I told him I was looking for my wife. I wasn't going to shoot him as the papers stated."

A strikingly good-looking young man, Fields seemed unaware of the seriousness of the charges he is facing.

—An article that appeared in the *California Eagle* but not in any white newspaper— the *Los Angeles Times,* the *Herald,* the *Examiner,* the *Mirror*—during the summer of 1956.

EPILOGUE

Margaret Bollinger became Mrs. Margie Galindo in 1957. She and Danny remained happily married, with a daughter and a son and a grandchild, until Danny's death just shy of his eighty-ninth birthday in the spring of 2010. Margie said that the two of them had just returned home from somewhere when Danny seized and fell in the foyer. There'd been no illness, no other symptoms.

Detective Danny Galindo, who received a commendation for this case, had indeed become the kind of detective who was sent behind the high stone walls where the rich and famous lived. He was the first detective on the scene when Sharon Tate and four others were murdered in Benedict Canyon in August 1969. And he was there the following night after Rosemary and Leno LaBianca were murdered with the same MO, miles away in the Los Feliz district. Danny's work as an investigator on the seven gruesome murders ordered by Charles Manson is documented in former prosecutor Vincent Bugliosi's bestseller, *Helter Skelter*.

Danny retired from the LAPD in 1977 and became an investigator for the State Bar of California, staying fifteen years. He was a public servant in the best sense of the word—a courageous warrior and the kind of cop everyone wishes that all cops would be. Above all, he wanted justice done. And he lived a justly rich and full life.

The same, alas, cannot be said of Todd Roark. His fate was the kind that tests the faith of those who believe in a moral universe. Upon his release from jail on his daughter Teri Denise's second birthday, Todd briefly lived with his girlfriend Queenie. A year later, having taken his name but not his marriage vows, Queenie gave birth to Toni. She put aside her singing aspirations and worked as a receptionist at Rocketdyne while going back to school and getting her teaching credential; by then Los Angeles schools were hiring "Negro" teachers in sufficient numbers to make it a viable career choice. Todd, however, remained shattered by the experience of having been falsely accused of rape. Unable to find suitable work, blocked by person or persons unknown from earning his private investigator's license, and in constant fear of coming across the white cops who he believed still had it out for him, he moved to Fresno and worked his father's farm. Toni said that whenever he came down to Los Angeles, he wore a fake beard as a disguise—and harbored deep animosity toward his old acquaintance Tom Bradley, the black cop turned city councilman who became L.A.'s longest-serving mayor, for never having come to Todd's aid.

Teri Denise grew up in a happy home in suburban San Diego, graduated from college, became a successful registered nurse and licensed public-health nurse, then a hospital administrator. She has been blessed with a long, happy marriage and two wonderful children (and now grandchildren). To her, Todd Roark was little more than an odd stranger. She'd seen him on only a few occasions after she'd reached young adulthood, and by then he was mostly blind from the diabetes that ultimately precipitated the strokes that ended his life in 1977 at age fifty-eight.

Not until she was eleven or twelve did Teri Denise know that her mother's husband, whom she called Daddy and who raised her exactly as if she'd always been his, was not her biological kin. Rummaging through a box in the attic one day, she'd chanced upon some newspaper clippings about a man named Todd Roark and rape. She'd begun asking questions that her mother, who'd apparently never gotten over the hurt of his affair with Queenie, wanted to avoid. So all Teri Denise knew about this mystery man who she discovered was her biological father was what she'd seen as fast as a flashbulb in those clips, and those were hurriedly replaced in the box and hidden away. On several occasions as she grew, a man in an old car would drive past her home or park out front, watching from afar. She was less frightened than intrigued, but still the effect was unsettling. And no wonder: until two years ago, Teri Denise believed that Todd Roark was a rapist. The revelation that another man, Willie Roscoe Fields, had confessed to the crimes upended everything she thought she knew about the man whose genes she carries, even if she wasn't, per se, his daughter. Her mother, Thelma, still angry about Todd's betrayal while she was pregnant with Teri Denise, must have had her reasons for not disabusing her daughter of the false belief. But it was too late to ask what they were. By the time Teri Denise heard the truth, her mother had passed on.

Poor Todd Roark. One can only imagine the pain and despair this man suffered the final twenty years of his life, having done nothing wrong beyond an ill-considered and ill-timed affair. Some men pay no price at all for such recklessness, but beyond the love of Queenie and Toni, this decorated American war hero who'd risen to the rank of first lieutenant—hardly ordinary for Negro soldiers then—paid more or less with a life sentence.

To the degree that any such colossal, cosmic unfairness can be balanced, it is only with the perpetrator's meeting a just end in prison, either by execution or natural causes. After all, the crimes of Willie Roscoe Fields were more serious and violent than those of the infamous Caryl Chessman, who was gassed in 1960. Aside from the rapes, kidnappings, and robberies, Fields had tried to blow Danny Galindo's head off and would have succeeded if not for the gun's misfiring.

But the L.A. district attorney had allowed Fields to plea the original nine counts down to two: the kidnappings of Margaret Bollinger and Charles Barker, neither of whom was harmed. The attempted murder and rapes were eliminated when Fields agreed to forgo the trial that could've sent him to death row. He made the right call, because even if he'd been acquitted, he was still on the hook to serve out in full the consecutive prison terms that went with the 1949 kidnapping and attempted-rape convictions whose probation he'd blown off in 1952.

No one in the Los Angeles District Attorney's office wanted to speculate why the DA back then had been willing to plead out Fields rather than going full bore with a capital case. This reluctance is understandable, given that no one from that era remains active. One rational guess about the reasoning is that the city's power brokers wanted to avoid bringing attention to these crimes. Another guess is that the DA didn't want to risk a defense lawyer informing a jury (even a white jury) that all those nonblack victims had misidentified a black perpetrator, and insisting that the same mistake was being made again. For either reason, a prosecutor might gladly have offered the plea on the two new counts, even if they were to run concurrently, knowing that the sentences imposed on the two earlier counts ran consecutively. Their cumulative effect was to earn Willie Roscoe Fields a term of twenty-five years plus twenty-five—ostensibly life for a man of thirty-four.

Then came a sea change. Just a year after Fields was sent to prison, a new California penal code section (3024) was adopted that reduced the minimum term of his incarceration to five years and made him (and thousands of other prisoners) eligible for parole after only two years. Yes, two years for crimes that ruined several lives, brought about the suicide of (at least) one young girl, and would have killed a police officer if not for a faulty pistol. That Fields was denied parole annually until 1970 still seems too little punishment, because that year a release date was set for 1971. The terms were that he was to remain on parole until 2032—obviously, long past the rest of his natural days—but after only eighteen months Willie Roscoe Fields was cut free with the sole restriction that he avoid drinking alcohol, which was considered the catalytic agent of his crimes. Of course, no one would ever know whether Fields was drinking as long as he avoided an arrest for drunk driving or public drunkenness.

His former parole officer, while not remembering Fields specifically, noted that that kind of punishment held in abeyance was common back then, even given that the governor was Ronald Reagan. (Berkeley students of that era will recall the movement for something called "prisoners' rights," which apparently entailed showing up at San Quentin and pretending that all prisoners were political prisoners.) "We thought more about rehabilitation then than we did punishment," he said, agreeing that it's a terrific idea in theory unless you were someone hurt by a bad guy's crimes, in which case the policies forced you to turn a cheek and forgive the person who ruined your life—though he hadn't asked for forgiveness. And Fields hadn't. Worse, he believed he had never hurt anyone and that all those women were his willing partners.

"Willie Fields," wrote the parole officer's supervisor in his agreement to terminate formal parole, "has done well in all areas of parole and has cooperated with the Parole Agent. Subject is a mild mannered, easy going person and it is felt that he does not constitute any danger to the free community in terms of criminal or anti social activities. For the above reasons, it is being recommended that Subject be discharged from parole supervision."

Upon his release from prison, Fields had had women fighting over him. Ruby, the wife he'd abandoned, had long before moved to San Francisco to be closer to him while he was in San Quentin, then had met and married another man. Now she wanted to divorce her husband and remarry Fields. A second woman also proposed to Fields, but the one he said yes to was a registered nurse in the East Oakland apartment building where he had taken up residence. She was his landlady, who between her rental income and excellent job was earning a nice income. As was Fields. Using the skills he'd developed in San Quentin's carpentry shop, he quickly landed a carpenter's job that, from day one, paid him the 2012 equivalent of $1,200 weekly.

The man who had destroyed so many lives was now married, a property owner, and, counting his wife's income, netting enough to be considered rich. One can envision Mr. and Mrs. Fields traveling frequently, driving the cars Fields had always coveted, entertaining often, and living well. Willie Roscoe Fields died peacefully in 1993 at age seventy—a dozen years longer than Todd Roark had.

That Fields apparently spent the rest of his days crime-free does not balance that Todd Roark went blind the year Fields was released from prison, and that as Todd's health continued to deteriorate, Fields grew more prosperous. It's true that bad things happen to good people; after all, even the best of us die. It's when good things happen to bad people that good people shake their heads.

AUTHOR'S NOTE

I met Danny Galindo in 1990, having set out to find a juicy true-crime story that had impact beyond its juiciness. For months I'd been asking LAPD cops and volunteers at the LAPD Historical Society for just such a story. None of them knew one and all suggested that I talk to detectives, retired or not. Alas, I didn't know any detectives, retired or not. But I figured that my uncle, Oscar Rothenberg, might. He was still practicing law then, and though he did little criminal work, he'd always had a keen ear for stories.

His somewhat discouraging observation was that Joseph Wambaugh, the former cop turned prolific true-crime author, had probably cultivated a network of detectives to feed him the best material. Still, my uncle said, he'd be happy to contact a friend at the LAPD. That turned out to be a propitious call.

Joseph P. Bonino was commanding officer of LAPD's records and identification division, and also the department's liaison to the FBI. Joe promised Oscar that he would try to arrange a lunch with a former detective who'd retired a dozen years earlier after thirty years on the force.

Joe called back to say that the man himself, Danny Galindo, had agreed to meet us.

Oscar and I drove to Parker Center in downtown L.A., named for the city's longest-serving police chief, a man who'd been hired to flush out the kind of corruption for which Los Angeles and its police department were justly known during the first half of the twentieth century—and amply portrayed in fiction ever since. Of course, corruption comes in many forms, not all of it pecuniary, so while the LAPD under Parker was no longer a cesspool of graft, neither was it free of controversy. I'm thinking particularly of steady complaints about the department from what was then called the Negro community.

I instantly liked Joe Bonino. He was charming, smart, and curious, and as we stood waiting for Danny, he seemed as excited as I was by the opportunity to hear tales from Galindo's storied career. What I remember vividly is the reaction on the faces of nearly everyone in the busy lobby when Danny walked in: all eyes followed him, and heads turned. The man was considered a living legend for his work on, if nothing else, the infamous Black Dahlia murder in 1947 and the Tate-LaBianca murders in 1969. He was then sixty-eight, I believe, but appeared at least two decades younger. He had a full head of white hair, a handsome, unlined face, the gait of an athlete, and clear eyes that focused with laser intensity. As Joe introduced me (and Oscar), I got the feeling Danny was sizing me up for whatever the criteria were that might open his vault of memories.

The four of us soon found ourselves at a Mexican restaurant east of downtown that Danny had chosen, and where, he said, a lot of Latino cops went. I thought he'd added the *Latino* qualifier as a way of bragging that the food was so good, even Mexicans ate there. Not till later did I understand this as a reference to how times had changed: unlike in his early days, plenty of Latinos were now on the force.

After the waitress took our orders, Danny began reeling off stories of murders and rapes (obviously leaving out the Black Dahlia and Manson cases, which had already been covered elsewhere). Many of these were interesting and compelling, but none were complex or important enough. Without question, he knew that, because just as I'd reached for the check and resigned myself to having not struck gold, here came a story he had been sitting on for thirty-four years.

When he finished (the punch line was "So then I married the girl"), he leaned back with a satisfied grin. The three of us sat silently until I began clapping, as did the other two.

I said, "That's the best true story I ever heard."

"Me, too," Joe added.

Same from Oscar.

All of us meant it, and all of us wondered why none of us had ever heard this before. Why hadn't it made big news? Or been a Wambaugh book?

Danny explained that in 1956, when these events took place, Los Angeles was in some ways as segregated a city as Selma, Alabama. What was covered in the so-called white press was different from what you could read in the black press, which consisted of weekly newspapers, not dailies. In the white press, stories about "Negroes" that might upset whites or make them fear for their safety or drive down property values or discourage yet more whites from making L.A. their new home were often ignored or spiked. Of all the people who knew this story, he said, only two come out looking good enough even to consider telling others.

The next day I phoned Danny to say that I very much wanted to write a book about the case. "I figured you would," he said, inviting me to his home, which was about an hour's drive from mine. When I arrived, he introduced me to his wife, his daughter, and his son before we went into his home office to talk further.

This was the first of at least a dozen trips to his home as he told me the story each time from a somewhat different point of view, adding details on details for which the previous day's or week's details were prerequisites. He did the same for conversations on the phone, though he seemed to hear a little better in person (all those years on the firing range without ear protection). His method offered some insight into the deductive brain of a first-class detective.

When he brought out his old .38 service revolver to show me, I knew we were getting somewhere. He also gave me a packet of clippings from a now defunct black newspaper that had covered the story, as well as clips from the white press, to illustrate the chasm in their coverage. Other documents included a crime study that he'd authored. He saved for last two photos, which are each worth ten thousand words: the cops in drag.

Over the ensuing year, I spent about fifty hours in person or on the phone with Danny Galindo, and a few hours with his wife. One time when I got to the house before Danny arrived, she graciously sat down with me and talked about the story. After Danny arrived and we were alone, I told him I could see why he'd fallen in love with her. He smiled in a way that could only be interpreted as a pat on his own back.

Anything Danny couldn't provide about the case was available in the city, county, and state archives, through the criminal courts, and on microfiche. What was most exciting about reading these old documents was how well they confirmed Detective Daniel Galindo's account of the events. He never said so, but I suspect he had something approaching a photographic memory.

So, given all that, why wasn't this book written twenty years ago?

Just when I'd felt ready to begin, I received and accepted a book offer that was too good to refuse. That was followed by another, and another. And so on. Years became a decade, then two. Danny's story may not have been on my computer, but it was never far from my mind.

As fate would have it, I found myself in early 2008 beginning what would become nearly three years investigating (as a volunteer, unpaid) the conviction of a young African man for rape the year before. My co-investigator was my uncle, and after we were certain that this Ghanaian who was rotting in a California prison had wrongly been convicted thanks to what we concluded was bad police work, an overzealous prosecutor, and an underzealous defense lawyer, we uncovered a veritable mountain of exculpatory evidence that the jury had never heard. The result was a seven-hundred-page petition for a writ of habeas corpus that is now wending its way through the judicial system.

During the investigation, I recognized how many dark parallels there were with Danny's story. Among other things, both revolved around rape and mistaken identifications. Since rape is in many ways the most grotesque of crimes, being falsely accused of it is in some ways nearly as grotesque. Once that angle of Danny's story was brought into sharper focus, thanks to my experience as a habeas investigator, I realized I couldn't not write the book.

This is a true story. Most of the dialogue, of course, is re-created or imagined based on what the parties, principally Danny, told me, as well as established facts, contemporaneous accounts, and interviews I conducted. A few of the names and other identifying details were altered, as per my agreements with sources, primarily victims. I also invented the names of some cops, one of whom is long deceased and whose real name Danny refused to tell me out of decency, insisting that this episode had changed the man for the better.

Writing this book, I learned a great deal about L.A., the city I grew up in. One of the things I thought I knew was that the city I grew up in was not a city where crosses were burned on lawns. But just the same, crosses were indeed burned on lawns, and firebombs were thrown through windows, in 1956. I learned good things, too, but nine years after the events rendered here, Watts exploded in violence. Those fires were not sparked in a vacuum.

—Joel Engel
January 2012

INDEX